ACTING IN
SOLIDARITY

Praise for *Acting in Solidarity:*

'*Acting in Solidarity* is the doing of theology at its best – engaging Christian learners in critical reflection, bodily involvement, and emotional investment over matters of faith and witness. Here creative and challenging drama moves us beyond the routinized pathologies of a dull religiosity. Instead, we become better Christians by literally assuming the realities different from our own. Isn't this what Jesus did to liberate the marginalized communities of his day?'

Dwight N. Hopkins, Professor of Theology at the University of
Chicago, is the author of *Being Human: Race, Culture, and Religion*

'Finally! – something that has thinking, questioning, reflecting Christians in mind. Dr Reddie has given us an invaluable resource for those of us who know that play, playfulness, wonder and imagination are for all ages – for all learners. This timely resource will assist us with the difficult and needed conversations which must take place if we are to grasp the new possibilities of the 21st century.'

Dr N. Lynne Westfield, Assistant Professor of Religious Education,
Drew University

'A really creative approach to real life questions and how they might be addressed through a re-reading of biblical passages, with helpful follow-up material and questions. This is an ideal resource for communities or groups of people to engage with – the range of subjects is comprehensive and does not skirt difficult issues, and there is enough humour to get you through the heavier stuff ... All round, thought-provoking and belly-splitting theological analysis.'

Dr Robert Beckford, Lecturer in African Diasporan Religions and
Cultures, University of Birmingham

ACTING IN SOLIDARITY

Reflections in Critical Christianity

Anthony G. Reddie

DARTON · LONGMAN + TODD

First published in 2005 by
Darton, Longman and Todd Ltd
1 Spencer Court
140–142 Wandsworth High Street
London SW18 4JJ

ISBN 0 232 52593 5

A catalogue record for this book is available from the British Library.

Designed and produced by Sandie Boccacci
Phototypeset in 11/14pt Minion
Printed and bound in Great Britain by
The Cromwell Press, Trowbridge, Wiltshire

To Noah
my nephew

*May the sentiments of this book be a pointer
to a better world that offers you so many
more possibilities than the often failed promises
that confronted your ancestors.*

Peace.

God bless you!

Contents

Acknowledgements

The finished product which you are holding disguises the pain, struggle, numerous amendments and, most importantly of all, the collaborative input of others which were all part of the process of this book achieving its final incarnation. *Acting in Solidarity* has my name on the front, but its arrival has been due to the hard work and support of a number of people.

In the first instance, I am indebted to Diane Johnson who bravely waded through numerous badly typed pieces of paper that represented my old manuscripts of sketches, dialogues and plays. She re-typed all my existing material, plus amending many of the newer pieces I had written. She went about the task with humour and diligence, and I am profoundly grateful. Her skills saved me incalculable amounts of time.

It would be remiss of me if I did not acknowledge the continuing support of the Research Centre at the Queens Foundation in particular and the whole Queens community in general. I continue to be thankful for the time and space afforded me by Queens to reflect and write.

If Queens are worthy of my thanks, then so too is the Methodist Church. The Pastoral Care and Christian Education, Racial Justice and Formation in Ministry sections of the Connexional Team of the Church deserve particular thanks for their moral and practical support.

Thanks are offered to Carol Troupe, my friend and confidante, for her searing honesty and consistent truth-telling. We all need people who will save us from the constant threat of arrogance and self-importance.

Thanks are extended to the many groups up and down the country with whom this material was trailed and piloted. Your honest reflections and interactions not only brought my 'flat' scripts to life, but also provided me with much-needed insights, which enabled me to write my reflections and construct study questions for future individuals and groups.

My penultimate thanks are reserved for the unseen and often unknown people within the many inner-city contexts of this country whose presence and commitment to life and faith have inspired me to write. It is often said that speaking your mind in the company of a writer is a seriously dangerous undertaking, as the writer *will* make use of what you have said, at some later date. All writers are, to some extent, emotional and psychological 'pick-pockets' and I am no different. To all those whose lives and stories have inspired me, I offer you my heartfelt thanks.

Finally, I would like to thank my family, particularly my parents, Lucille and Noel Reddie, but not forgetting my siblings, Richard, Christopher and Sandra, plus Uncle Mervin and Auntie Lynette, and best of all, my little nephew Noah. You are all special people in my life, and without you I would be a lesser human being.

Introduction

So why this book?

I began writing Christian drama whilst in my first year at University. It would be much too narcissistic an exercise for me to recount the tortuous journey of those first doubtful creative efforts at this juncture,[1] but in many respects, my discovery of creative writing in the form of Christian drama was to be the turning point in my life. Prior to that sudden moment in 1985, when I wrote my first dramatic piece, I had struggled to give expression to an inquiring and complex inner world that lay dormant within me.

I was often chided in those days for being much too quiet and introspective (like such character traits were a crime). I am told (by my Mother, who is an unimpeachable guardian in these matters) that I was a solitary and thoughtful child. As the eldest child of Caribbean migrants (who often became the cultural and social guinea-pig for the family – I was, for example, the first to enter a primary school in Britain), I was constantly aware of my 'otherness'.[2]

The defence mechanism I developed to counter the continuing sense of being 'other' in the dichotomous world of belonging within both a Black perspective (of my family) and a White one (of industrial East Bowling, Bradford) was to withdraw into myself.[3]

For many years during my middle to late teens I occupied a cultural and social space that found expression in being on the 'edge of things', peering on or looking in. I rarely permitted myself the luxury of 'becoming' and 'belonging'. I often wondered whether the world as I interpreted it from within my enclosed and detached interior was the same one that others were experiencing. I wondered whether I was simply odd or perhaps intuitively gifted? I guess that the intervening years have proved that both of these labels can be applied to me, although the degree to which these differing perspectives can be seen in me, is perhaps a matter best judged by others.

What I remember most distinctly is the sense that the world as detailed in the words and the sentiments of people, and the actions that then gave expression to these thoughts, were often wildly different. From my vantage point of sitting on the edge, I witnessed the countless, casual incidences of people often expressing one particular set of thoughts, and then acting or behaving in a manner that seemed to totally disprove or contradict the former.

Nowhere was this seemingly habitual discrepancy (at best) or hypocrisy (at worst) more glaringly displayed than within the Christianity to which I was exposed. Time and again I witnessed people say one thing and do another. Whether within the realms of pastoral care (there always seemed to be a clear divide between those who deserved support and those who did not), or in ethics (the litany of racialised incidents are too numerous to mention), most of the Christian people I knew seemed to exude a glaring divided nature.

As I witnessed this ongoing phenomenon, I wondered whether it was the people themselves who were at fault, or whether it was the rather unhelpful legacy of Christian faith and tradition as bequeathed to us by our forebears that was to blame. The vantage point of being on the edge of things enabled me to reflect and document the many incidents of cognitive dissonance within the lives of Christian believers. From that first moment of writing way back in the mid 1980s, through my subsequent training and development as a religious educator and theologian, I have returned at periodic moments to the format of drama in order to bring to life concerns and issues that have troubled me.

So why Christian drama?

I have often resorted to drama due to its dialectical or conversational manner. By this I mean that drama involves the use of different characters or voices in a particular situation or context – often one of conflict. This can help to bring particular ideas or concerns to life. I have often used drama as a medium to address issues of concern within Christianity for a variety of reasons.

First, drama is a readily accessible medium for people to interact with one another and with the subject/topic of concern that is at the heart of the dramatic exercise. Educators have long asserted that drama provides a means for interaction and involvement which leads to greater engagement for the learner.[4] I have been concerned to find a means by which ordinary Christians can be enabled to enter into a process of teaching and learning in which their presence and interaction is central to the overall educational enterprise. Drama requires that people are actively engaged in a process of discovery.

Second, by using drama, I was able to explore a range of ideas and concerns in a way that would be very difficult in conventional prose. Drama usually comes alive by means of conflict and intellectual and emotional struggle. Characters meet, engage, dialogue and seek truth within the confines of the drama. Often, when I wanted to gain insight into the alternative perspective to the one I might personally hold, it has proved useful to create a short piece of drama. Drama can bring to life a range of voices that can articulate perspectives radically different from one's own. Drama can bring to life voices which have an integrity and a truth of their own – often a truth that is beyond the immediate scope of the writer who conceived the piece in the first instance.

Acting in Solidarity represents the edited, collected works of this process of theological exploration by means of drama over a period of several years. This book is not a detailed analysis of the utility of drama as a means of theological exploration.[5] Rather, this is a collection of work that seeks to address a range of concerns within Christian life and experience through a dramatic format.

Over the past decade or so, since I began my work as a religious educator and theologian, I have used these dramatic pieces as a way of enabling learners (often in groups), whether in formal or informal contexts, to reflect upon particular issues or concerns within Christian life and the life of the Church. Be it within the setting of a theological college or in a more informal gathering such as a Bible study or fellowship group, these pieces have been used to stimulate discussion and critical inquiry. In writing these pieces, I have been more concerned with creating lively, humorous slices of action that address a number of issues or queries for those interacting with them. Less emphasis has been given to creating 'great drama' (however that nebulous concept is defined), although one's pride as an author usually ensures that every effort is made to construct something that is worthy of carrying one's name.

Acting in solidarity?

The collected works that make up this book share a number of common themes. I had not realised the unifying thread that permeates the many pieces I have written until I was asked one day by a number of partici-pants at a workshop I was leading to provide them with some material to assist them in their roles as trainers. As I trawled through my back catalogue, I came across a number of pieces that seemed to hark back to my own formative experiences in the Church. From my vantage point of sitting on the edge of things, I had long been critical of a number of existing concepts within Christian theology and practice.

On the rare occasions when I had ventured to share my concerns with others, the result had not always proved a positive or enlightening affair. The reaction of some of my fellow travellers in the faith was akin to the conventionality that often abounds in many Christian communi-ties. Jeff Astley has commented on the conventions that exist in many churches with respect to issues of faith development in their attendees. The majority of church attendees tend to be located at a mid point in the conventional scale for faith development.[6]

Having spent many years harbouring my subversive interior clouds of critical thought and doubt, I was delighted to find that a number of people have responded enthusiastically to my concerns when exposed to the various pieces in this book, when used in a workshop or a class-room format. In attempting to write in solidarity with those who are in critical dialogue with Christianity, these pieces cover areas that are usually ignored by traditional theology and Christian drama books.

The pieces in this book, which begin with my own experience as their first point of departure, are written in solidarity with those who are seeking a critical form of Christianity in which they can believe. It is an overarching form of faith that does not constrict, immobilise or oppress those who adhere to it or those with whom it comes into contact. Neither does it seek to create damaging dichotomies between those who might be described as 'them' and those who are the 'us' – whoever these might be.

Acting in Solidarity is (hopefully) a humorous and interactive ex-ercise in critical Christianity. The various pieces are small, unresolved case studies in aspects of Christian theology and practice that might be seen as problematic or challenging for many people, particularly those who might describe themselves as marginalised, whether on the grounds of 'race', gender, poverty, sexuality or geography. They are, in effect, discussion or conversation starters, and not densely thought-through theological treatises. The various pieces in *Acting in Solidarity* are an interactive means of 'kick-starting' a process of theological exploration for individuals and groups of all ages, cultures, communities and contexts.

The work has been separated into a number of sections. These are 'Biblical Re-telling', 'Pastoral Care and Ministry', 'Racial Justice and Black Theology' and 'Ethics and Action'. The short pieces of drama have been created, along with some short reflections and follow-up questions, in order that participants can think and reflect upon issues of faithful living in an active and dynamic way.

How to Use this Material

The material in this book has been written primarily for educational and theological purposes, not necessarily artistic ones. That is not to say that a great deal of thought has not gone into the writing of the various pieces in order that they might be effective, challenging, authentic and enjoyable pieces of drama. The main aim in providing this work, however, is to provide a method for enabling people (usually in groups) to be active participants in a dramatic process of theological reflection.

I am aware that many people are afraid of drama and will claim, seemingly with great delight, that they 'cannot act if their lives depended upon it'. Well, the material in this book, although challenging on occasions, does not require participants to be proficient actors. The sketches do not require any extensive preparation, nor is there any need for props or costumes. I am not even assuming that people will learn the lines in the various sketches. The following notes are a kind of dramatic educational 'process' that will enable groups to work with the material in a manner that will help them to get the most out of it, without any assumptions on my part as to their acting ability.

The process

1. Make copies of the pre-sketch reflections for each participant in the group. Read through the reflections quietly, but there should be no discussion of the reflections before the sketch is performed.
2. Before you perform a sketch, decide who will play the various parts in the script. Try and ensure that people are playing against type – that is, people should be playing characters that are *the least like them*.
3. Split those who are not performing in the sketch into groups. The number of groups should be linked to the number of characters in

the sketch. Depending on the overall size of your group (performers and bystanders), you may need to 'double-up' (i.e. more than one group of people representing a particular character). So, for example, in *Bestseller* there are two main characters (Isaiah and the Literary Agent); I would suggest that you split those who are not performing into two groups, each one representing a character in the sketch. If you have a large group, you can 'double-up' as I have suggested earlier.

4. Some sketches have minor characters (bit players with limited speaking parts). You may want to assign a group(s) to these characters, or you may feel that there is insufficient material with which a group can identify as they observe and follow the action from the wings, so to speak.

5. Perform each sketch at least twice.[1] You can vary the people playing the different parts (they should be allocated a character group as well). Ask the people in the different groups, in addition to concentrating on the drama as it unfolds, (a) to consider how they feel as they see their character perform in the sketch, and (b) to compare the actions and personality of the character to their own. Is the character with whom you are identifying like you or not? How are you similar (if at all)? Do you like them? Do you empathise with what they are saying and how they are behaving?

6. The stage directions and scene details are only suggestive. You can simply get people to read the parts without any great attempt to recreate the setting in which the action is taking place; but obviously, the more attempts you make in this respect, the more effective will be the resulting performances.

7. There may be occasions when you need someone to read the stage directions in order that the group participants can follow the action when the lead characters are not speaking.

8. Ensure that only those who are performing in the sketch have sight of the script before it is performed for the first time. A major element in the learning is that initial element of surprise.

9. After the second performance (possibly with different players), ask *all* participants (i.e. those directly 'acting' and those who have reacted in their groups) to remain silent for a few moments.

Taking time out

Immediately following the performance of the sketch, all participants are advised to spend a few minutes reflecting upon the events they have just witnessed. What are their immediate feelings and thoughts? How do they feel about the drama that has just taken place? Participants are encouraged to connect with their feelings for a few moments.

This opportunity for 'time out' is to enable participants to reflect individually on any feelings that may have emerged in the performance of the sketch – be it feelings of anger, frustration, bemusement, joy or surprise. This need not be a very long period, perhaps a minute or so.

Helping people to get out of role

Following the silence, ask *all* participants to close their eyes and inhale deeply. Then ask them to breathe out slowly and then, in unison, to count down from 10 to 1. When the countdown is completed, invite all participants to open their eyes and stretch and move around for a few moments.

10. After allowing the participants to come out of role, ask individuals to go into their character groups. Ask them in their groups to share their reflections on questions (a) and (b) raised in No. 5 above. Ask each group to record some of their reflections on flip-chart paper. How different are these reflections from the behaviour of their character in the sketch? Who could identify with the character and who could not? What emerged from the group discussion?
11. Ask the different groups to share their reflections with one another. How do the different perspectives compare?
12. Make copies of the post-sketch reflections for all participants. Invite individuals to read through the reflections.
13. Provide some time for discussion of both the pre-sketch and the post-sketch reflections.
14. When the aforementioned has been completed, invite all participants to consider the study questions that follow the post-sketch reflections.

Note: Depending upon time, you may wish to omit Nos. 1 and 14 – i.e. go straight into the sketch and then into the post-sketch reflections, but omitting the study questions.

Strategies for undertaking drama

In order to get the best out of the material in this book, it is imperative that participants are encouraged to enter seriously into the dramatic context of each sketch. Taking the context seriously does not necessarily mean being serious or behaving in a fashion that precludes humour or laughter. One of the most effective ways of raising serious issues is by way of humour.

The dramatic sketches at the heart of this approach to theological reflection demand that participants are willing to enter into the 'internal logic' of the sketch. By internal logic, I am referring to a process in which the participant takes seriously the perspective of the character they are playing, and imbues the role with a sense of seriousness. This mode of behaviour is not unlike that demanded of participants in Groome's[2] or Berryman's[3] respective educational approaches to Practical theology.

Internal logic is the sense that the world as defined by the sketch, no matter how improbable or absurd, is in some sense real and to be taken seriously, the sense of asking participants to suspend their critical, realist judgements, in order to enter into the internal logic and dynamic of a piece of drama.

Creating a positive learning environment

Perhaps the greatest responsibility of the leaders/facilitators is to provide an environment in which participants can be enabled to ask critical questions of Christianity and some of the underlying theology that underpins many of the accepted norms of the faith. Whilst I am not pretending to be neutral in terms of my own personal interpretation of the faith and the resulting practice of the Church, my interest in writing this book is not to impose my particular perspectives on others. Rather, my intention in creating this work is to challenge people to reflect critically on the Christian faith and the working out of that faith within their lives.

Having used these pieces in a wide variety of settings over several years, I can attest to the way in which subtle nuances and multiple meanings and interpretations emerge from the repeated performance of any piece.

Prior to each piece there are some short reflections explaining why it was written, what areas it covers (what I am trying to do or say) and how it might be explored and used. Following the piece are some further reflections that raise some of the issues and concerns from the previous occasions when this piece has been used with different groups. As with my earlier books, *Growing into Hope*, the material in this book can be adapted or amended in order to suit the particular needs and concerns of individuals or groups. Please do not be afraid to change anything.

Following each sketch there are a series of questions inviting participants to reflect upon their involvement in the dramatic piece and to consider the implications of these reflections for Christian discipleship and action. It is important that participants are encouraged to think critically about the relationship between the characters in the drama, the resulting theological reflections and their own experiences, which are also informed by the Bible. How do they respond to the challenges posed by the drama and the issues that arise from it?

Creating a positive learning environment requires that the facilitators create a positive and affirming setting in which there is trust, sharing and encouragement. The purpose of the 14-point (educational) process I have outlined is to help in the creation of a learning environment that will assist all learners.

Creating a supportive and affirming learning environment is of crucial importance not least because of the nature of the material in the book. The material in *Acting in Solidarity* does not provide neat, easy solutions to some of the major issues in life, nor does it attempt to gloss over concerns that are often inherently contradictory, complex and sometimes disturbing. A number of the pieces, for example, deal with issues of 'race', injustice, imbalances of power and discrimination.

Similarly, some of the pieces deal with cross-cultural dialogue or, to be more accurate, our failure to communicate with one another. Perhaps most controversially, a couple of the pieces I have written dare to critique aspects of Black culture – issues which often get overlooked, due in part to the fact that Black and other marginalised people are so often victimised and demonised that they become insular and defensive, and thereby find it difficult to criticise aspects of their lives, outlooks and behaviour.

Due to some of the challenging issues and themes that are present in the book, it is essential that facilitators are mindful of the feelings and thoughts that might emerge from the encounter between participants' experiences and the dramatic learning material with which they are performing and reflecting.

I hope you enjoy engaging with *Acting in Solidarity*. It is my hope that these various pieces will stimulate critical Christian thinking and lead to renewed praxis in solidarity with all those who feel themselves neglected and overlooked, for whatever reason.

BIBLICAL RE-TELLING

In this section I am interested in assisting individuals and groups to look afresh at particular passages or sections of the Bible. The Bible offers numerous challenges and opportunities, many of which get lost because of the way in which we often approach this book. I suspect that one of the reasons we miss the most challenging and radical elements of the Bible is due to our familiarity with it. We think we know it very well. In actual fact we often fail to realise how distant from it we are. We are not as well informed about the Bible as we often imagine. These collections of writings, written over a long period of history, are not recently constructed texts, as we sometimes believe them to be.

What often confronts us, therefore, is a huge contradiction. On the one hand, as Christian believers, often nurtured within the life of the Church, we feel that we know what the Bible is about. We read it and feel that we know God. Our familiarity leads us to 'domesticate' the Bible – to make it safe, palatable and comfortable for our times. God becomes one of us, who can be used to justify our prejudices, boundaries and views of the world.[1] Yet on the other hand, our distance from the times in which the Bible was written often leads us to (at best) misunderstand what the Bible says or (at worst) to distort and misrepresent God as understood in the pages of Scripture.

One of the ways in which biblical scholars, theologians and educators have attempted to respond to these issues has been by 'recontextualising' the Bible. By this I mean trying to re-tell the various stories of the Bible in another setting or situation from the one in which they were first written. This new setting can unsettle us – it can put us off our guard and disturb our complacency. Suddenly, what we thought we knew is pushed aside in the face of a new version with which we are unfamiliar. This forces us into new ways of thinking and so leads to new learning. Writers such as Wangerin,[2] Coles,[3] McCrary[4] and Anderson and Maddox[5] have all attempted to put Bible passages into completely new settings and forms from the ones in which they were first set, in order that they should speak to us in different ways for our present situation.

The following section is a collection of relatively short sketches or skits that attempt to disturb our complacencies around some of the more famous (or in one case, not so famous) stories in the Bible. I wanted to write in a very abstract or absurdist way, mainly to cut any relationship between what we think we know and what might emerge from a completely new approach to a particular story.

A variety of scholars have identified the ways in which insight can emerge from seemingly foolish or even absurdist approaches to viewing reality.[6] Kenneth Leech, who has written about mental ill health and pastoral care, challenges us to look differently at how we assess people with mental ill health, as often, in the midst of their condition, they speak more truth than those who might be termed 'normal' (whatever that is).[7]

A number of years ago, I was a member of an amateur Christian drama group, with a number of friends from the University of Birmingham Methodist Society.[8] One of our stated aims in our writing and performing was to break the 'cosy middle-class conformity' of Christian drama. To our youthful minds, too much Christian drama available at that time seemed totally oblivious to the developments in mainstream comedy in particular. The claims of the Goons, Monty Python, Spike Milligan, the Young Ones and Black Adder (no Black artists here, but that's another story!) often went unnoticed.

A major part of our difficulty when presenting biblical material in a new guise is our often rigid insistence on trying to tie up all the loose ends. Christian drama often attempts to re-tell the story in such a conventional manner in order that the obvious message and meaning (and these things are always obvious, aren't they?) always comes through. I have decided, drawing upon my past experiences, that one of the best means of assisting people to critically engage with reality (drawing upon the work of Leech[9] and Boal[10]) is to dispense with the usual and normal ways of looking at events or situations. So gone are the seemingly conventional attempts to 'tell the story'.

Instead, I have opted for sometimes strange – some might even say downright foolish – approaches to the re-setting of Bible stories. One might even argue that such an approach to re-reading the Bible and reflecting theologically is an essential component in telling the good news of Jesus. For, to paraphrase the sentiments of the writer of the first letter to the Corinthians, what we preach may appear foolish to those who consider themselves learned in the affairs of the world.[11]

The material in this section is based upon a series of sketches. Prior to each sketch are some reflections outlining what I am trying to do or address in this piece and how it might be used. Following each sketch are some additional reflections that have arisen from its use with groups and individuals across the country. These are intended to assist in the process of enabling individuals and groups to reflect critically upon the issues that have arisen in the sketch. Following each sketch are some questions for further discussion and action.

Bestseller

Opening reflections

In one of the introductory sessions run for our post-graduate students on the MA in Applied Theological Studies at the college where I work,[1] a number of us were asked by one of the Biblical Studies tutors to identify our favourite book of the Old Testament. The two most popular choices amongst the many participants in the room were Isaiah and the Psalms. I opted for the Book of Isaiah. Within Isaiah, my favourite 'text within the text' is chapter 53.

One of the most memorable experiences of my early twenties was co-leading an Easter meditation run by a number of Birmingham University Methodist Society (Meth.Soc) students at one of our annual Easter vacation missions in a local church in the West Midlands. The combination of music, silence and the spoken words of chapter 53 made for a very powerful and emotional impact. As a Black British person living in the UK, I identified with the sentiments and the emotional context of that passage completely.

Why was and is chapter 53 so pivotal for so many Black people and other marginalised people in the world? For many of them, the passage taps into their experiences of struggle and oppression.[2] The passage in Isaiah has generated a great deal of debate for many years. Some have said that the person mentioned in the passage is Jesus. It foretells the sacrifice and suffering he would undergo in order that humankind might be reconciled to God. On the other hand, others have argued that we should not bring our knowledge of later events as described in the New Testament (particularly the life, death and resurrection of Jesus shown in the four Gospels), and use them to understand what an earlier passage might have meant. Could previous authors writing long before Jesus' birth be really thinking about him when they wrote this passage?

Another question many people have asked concerns the author of the whole Book of Isaiah. Some people believe that one person wrote all 66 chapters; others state that more than one author wrote the book. As the book seems to divide into two sections, the differences between the two parts (part 1 is chapters 1–39, part 2 is chapters 40–66) would seem to indicate that a number of different writers wrote the book, at different times and in different places.

Aside from the specific questions asked of the text by specialist biblical scholars, I want to concentrate my thoughts for a few moments on the particular questions asked of Isaiah by those who have been marginalised and oppressed by people with power. Thinking in terms of chapter 53, what does it mean to be an individual, solitary 'suffering servant' who becomes the 'scapegoat' for the anger and deep-seated vitriol of the many?[3]

Within Black theological thought, a number of writers have located within the suffering of Jesus (whose struggle and ultimate death, it is believed, is foreseen by the writer of this text) a sense of divine solidarity with their own historical and contemporary experiences of unjustified and unmerited suffering. Scholars such as Douglas,[4] Cone[5] and Terrell,[6] to name but a few, have all explored the theological significance for Black people of Jesus' suffering on the cross, believed (by virtually all Black Christians) to be foretold in Isaiah 53.

Writing with reference to this theme, Terrell states:

> Yet the tendency among Black people has been to identify wholly with the suffering of Jesus because the story made available to them – Jesus' story – tells of his profound affinity with their plight. Like the martyrs, they are committed to him because his story is their story. Jesus' death by crucifixion is a prototype of African Americans' death by *circumscription*.[7]

This radical identification with the undeserved suffering of an innocent individual has exerted a powerful hold on the imagination of many Black people and other marginalised and oppressed groups in the world.[8]

In this sketch I wanted to 'play' with the idea of the writer of Isaiah as a modern-day author trying to get his/her work published. How would they go about trying to 'sell' a piece of work that is provocative, challenging and very, very long? Does it matter who was the author?

And given its length, are there particular parts of the text that speak to us more than others? Are some parts of it more important or true than others? Consider these thoughts as you perform *Bestseller*.

———◄◦►———

Bestseller

(The scene is inside a posh office. Sitting at one end of the stage is a literary agent. We see him/her flicking through a very thick manuscript. After a few seconds, enter a secretary.)

SECRETARY: Your eleven o'clock appointment has arrived. Shall I send Isaiah through?

LITERARY AGENT: *(Without looking up)* Yes, send him through.

SECRETARY: Thank you, Sir/Madam.

(Exit secretary ... enter Isaiah. He approaches L.A., quite nervous. Stands motionless for a while.)

L.A.: *(Looking up)* Ah ... Isaiah. Please take a seat.

(Isaiah does so.)

L.A.: *(Begins to flick through the long manuscript)* Well, Mr ... Isaiah. I must say, I'm particularly impressed with this ... *(Places manuscript in his palm and pretends to weigh it in his hands)* ... very thorough piece of work. Absolutely wonderful.

ISAIAH: I'm glad you like it.

L.A.: Like it? Like it? I love it. This is a work of pure genius, Isaiah. This is going to be a bestseller. A Booker Prize winner. A Pulitzer Prize. We are going to be rich.

ISAIAH: *(Feeling more relaxed)* I'm relieved you enjoyed reading it. I was a little on edge just now. I thought you might not like it, but now I've heard ...

L.A.: *(Interrupting Isaiah)* But there are a few problems which will need ironing out before we can publish.

ISAIAH: *(Thrown momentarily)* Ah ... A few problems?

L.A.: Just a few. Nothing much, just a few teething difficulties.

ISAIAH: Right.

L.A.: Let's make a start. First thing, Isaiah ... The length.

ISAIAH: The length?

L.A.: *(Begins to weigh the manuscript out in the palm of one hand again)* A bit on the heavy side, huh? Trifle long, wouldn't you say?

ISAIAH: Hmmm … I don't know.

L.A.: Sixty-six long chapters. A bit extreme, don't you think?

ISAIAH: Yes, but …

L.A.: I'm not saying it's boring … Well, not that boring. Boringish. It has boring tendencies. A strong essence of boring, but not boring as such.

ISAIAH: So what are you saying?

L.A.: I think we could lose a few chapters.

ISAIAH: How many?

L.A.: Just a few.

ISAIAH: What chapters did you have in mind?

L.A.: *(Hedging)* Well, this is only a hunch, OK? I mean, don't take this as Gospel … *(Thinks for a moment)* Gospel? Now that's a good idea … *(Picks up a Dictaphone and begins to speak into it)* Memo to secretary. Idea for four connecting stories. About God. Or at least someone who claims he's God. Going to call it *Gospel.* Or something like that. Need to find writers. Reliable and speedy with it. Must follow this up … *(Quickly remembering himself)* Now, Isaiah. I could be wrong … but … *(Takes a deep breath, then begins to speak very quickly)* We could lose half of chapter 5, 'Woes and Judgements'. We could do without chapter 6, 'Isaiah's Commission'. *(Looks at Isaiah)* … I don't think we need to hear that. We'll take your word for it. Then we can lose chapter 11, 'The Branch from Jesse', chapter 15, 'A Prophecy Against Moab'. Prophecy doesn't sell anymore. Chapters 17, 18 and 19, more prophecy. Cut 23, lose 24, edit 28, lose 31, 32, 33, 34 and 40. Obliterate 46 and completely scrub chapters 58 to 63 … But chapter 42 I like. 'The Servant of the Lord'. Nice touch. Very moving. Do you have any questions, Isaiah?

ISAIAH: Hmmm … You've certainly done a hatchet job on my work.

L.A.: Now I can understand how you feel, Isaiah, but don't see it as a hatchet job. More … creative editing. Overall, I like it. Great, super, smashing.

ISAIAH: Alright, if you're sure. Was there anything else?

L.A.: *(Pause)* Yes … Just one thing. I don't know how to bring it up. You see, Isaiah … we're having a little problem with the authorship of this work.

ISAIAH: What?

L.A.: It's nothing, really ... It's just that there are a few inconsistencies to be dealt with ... This is all your own work?

ISAIAH: *(Suspiciously)* Are you saying otherwise?

L.A.: *(Nervously)* Well ... there are three things that lead us at Judean Publishing Incorporated to question the authorship of this work.

ISAIAH: Go on.

L.A.: First, there is the handwriting.

ISAIAH: What about it?

L.A.: It changes as the story progresses. Changes quite a lot, actually. It's almost as if different people had written specific sections.

ISAIAH: My hand was hurting me. It takes it out of you, writing 66 chapters. I changed pens nine times and wrote left-handed from chapter 39 onwards.

L.A.: Then there's the dramatic inconsistencies in the spelling. It goes from being quite tight and organised, through to being absolutely slap-dash and pathetic near the end.

ISAIAH: My brain was getting tired. I lost my dictionary. Someone nicked my thesaurus.

L.A.: Then finally, there is the writing style itself. Let me read you an extract from chapter 53 ... *(Finds the relevant page in the manuscript)* 'Who hath believed our report? And to whom is the arm of the Lord revealed? He shall grow up before him as a tender plant, and as a root out of a dry ground: He hath no form nor attractiveness, and when we shall see him, there is no beauty that we should desire him.' Now let me read you an extract from chapter 3 ... *(Finds the relevant page again. Looks up and down and frowns.)* 'For, Behold the Lord, the Lord of hosts, doth take away from Jerusalem and from Judah the staff ... blah blah blah ...' *(Looks up at Isaiah)* Two different types of writing! Isaiah?

ISAIAH: Hmmm ... I ran out of caffeine?

L.A.: You certainly did. The later chapters read like potential Booker Prize material. The earlier stuff, chapters 1 to 39, are a bit dry. What do you have to say for yourself, Isaiah?

ISAIAH: I have a confession to make.

L.A.: Go on, I'm listening.

ISAIAH: I didn't write it all by myself.

L.A.: You don't say ...

ISAIAH: I had a little help.

L.A.: Go on.

ISAIAH: My brothers helped me.

L.A.: And who are they?

ISAIAH: Isaiah.

L.A.: I know your name already. What I meant was, what are your brothers called?

ISAIAH: Isaiah.

L.A.: You and your brothers are all called Isaiah?

ISAIAH: Family tradition.

L.A.: I see … And all of you wrote the book? Which bit did you write?

ISAIAH: Chapters 1 to 39.

L.A.: It figures … *(Gets to his feet)* Now, let me think … *(Dashes back to his desk and picks up the telephone)* Get me the Chief Executive, I've just thought of a great idea. The Isaiah Boys. The Writing Brothers. The Brothers Who Write. Get in touch with Hebrew Films Corporation. Tell them they can have the film rights to *Isaiah, the Movie*. It will make great TV. It will run for years, *Isaiah, the Soap*. What's that again? The brothers thing won't work? … *(Puts down the telephone)* Isaiah, call your brothers. I want a word.

ISAIAH: Anything you say.

L.A.: Fame and fortune, here we come. They will never forget this book. It will be read in hundreds of years' time. Just one thing … we'll forget the Writing Brothers thing. As far as anyone is concerned, this is all your own work, *capiche*?

ISAIAH: But what about my brothers?

L.A.: Not to worry, they can write other things. They will make great ghost-writers. We've got this client called Jeremiah. Great bloke, but his writing needs some work. Time for your brothers to step up to the plate. He's a bit on the serious side and his writing isn't that hot. I think your brothers can add a little pep to his work. But that's for the future. For here and for now, we are looking at a bestseller. Any questions, Isaiah?

ISAIAH: *(Bewildered)* Hmmmm. No. Anything you say!

THE END

———◆———

Post-sketch reflections

The sketch you have just performed or watched is of course a completely made-up bit of nonsense. It goes without saying that nothing
like this ever happened. One of the things I wanted to explore in writing
the piece is to ask a very modern question. How would the composition
of something like the Book of Isaiah be accomplished in our present
age? At a time when J. K. Rowling's *Harry Potter* series is breaking all
records, how would the author or authors of this huge book go about
getting that work published, particularly given the fact that it was not
written as a piece of entertainment? Given that the book has some very
harsh things to say about the people who might have first read it, many
of the participants who have engaged with the sketch and reflected on
it, doubted whether it would be possible to get that kind of work
published today.

A great deal of the writing in Isaiah is seen as a direct lead-in to the
later ministry of Jesus. Just as Jesus challenged injustice and called for
people to turn away from their old ways of living and behaving, so many
years before Jesus' appearance, the author(s) of Isaiah were doing something similar. There are a number of things to note about this book:

According to many African scholars, there are many parallels
between the problems that faced Israel (which the writer(s) of this book
comment upon) and those which face many countries in modern-day
Africa.[9] They argue that when a country is confronted by immense
problems arising from globalisation and has numerous internal
problems and difficulties, that country must acknowledge its need for
God to guide and direct them. What are some of the problems facing
Africa at this time?

Many Black scholars have argued that some of the questions people
have asked about the history or background of the text are secondary
ones.[10] Whilst it is important to know something of the history and
background to certain books and passages in the Bible, what is more
important is how we act and behave, having read these works.[11] What
action will reading the Bible lead us into? For the many people (largely
of African descent) who have experienced great hardship and material
poverty, the Book of Isaiah, particularly chapter 53, has proved an
inspiration.

Despite many struggles and much opposition (look through the book again and make a list of the difficulties the author(s) face), the person(s) telling the story never give up. They refuse to be silent in the face of the different things they are witnessing.[12]

Because it is easier (perhaps even preferable) to identify with one man who is inspired by God to speak up and make a difference rather than several people, many of the Black and other peoples who have engaged with this sketch have tended to favour the idea of there being one author.

For many who have engaged with this sketch, chapters 53, 61 and 63 are key sections of the whole book. The key to their importance lies in their identification with Jesus' later ministry. The author(s) seem to be promising the coming of one who will change the whole situation in which this nation (and later the whole world) finds itself. For all people who are struggling in this present world, this promise is a very powerful and seductive one.

Follow-up questions

Read selected parts of Isaiah, particularly chapters 53, 61 and 63. Having read these sections of Isaiah and having reflected on the sketch, consider the following questions:

- How might the promise of someone coming in the future to change all the injustice and hatred in the world be important for some people who are presently being oppressed or are persecuted?
- Does it matter to you whether one person wrote the whole of Isaiah, or whether it was written by a number of people (many scholars say three people) over a long period of time? If yes, then why? If not, then why not?
- The person who is spoken of in chapter 53 is described as one who takes on themselves all the pain and struggles of others. What would you say to those who might describe this kind of person as a 'mug' or just plain gullible for taking on this kind of role? How would you feel about taking on this kind of role? Is it 'part and parcel' of being a Christian?
- Think back to the discussion in the sketch about the size of this book – which parts of Isaiah strike you as being most important and why?

- If you had to edit the book (because of limits of space), which parts would you keep because they sum up what the whole thing is all about?
- For many people, the Book of Isaiah is the key section of the Old Testament. If there is one thing you would take from this book, what would it be and why?
- Having reflected on the Book of Isaiah, what will you do next? What action will reading Isaiah lead you into?

In the Psychiatrist's Chair

Opening reflections

The story of Moses has always intrigued me. One of the reasons I have always identified with Moses is due, to some extent, to his status as 'unpromising material'. On the face of it, Moses' formative years do not seem to fit him for the tremendous work he would undertake at a later point in his life. Moses is born into difficult circumstances (see the Book of Exodus, chapter 2). I am sure that there are many of us who might describe ourselves as being 'unpromising material'. Due to his heroic actions as the leader of a liberation movement, many Black and marginalised peoples have identified with Moses. Some Black theologians have even identified Moses as being a Black person of African ancestry.[1]

The renowned African American singer Isaac Hayes, one of the most popular singers of the late 1960s and early 1970s, even dubbed himself a latter-day 'Black Moses' due to his prophecy-like utterances on record. Long before Hayes, women such as Nanny of the Maroons (an eighteenth-century Jamaican national hero) and Harriet Tubman (a nineteenth-century African American hero) were seen as Moses-like figures due to their leadership qualities. Who are the Moses-like figures in our present age?[2] Where are we looking to find these people? What are we looking for? I invite you to consider some of these questions as you act out and engage with the following sketch.

————◄o►————

In the Psychiatrist's Chair

(We see a man standing/sitting centre stage. We hear a bell ringing. A receptionist walks on stage.)

RECEPTIONIST: Dr Gruber ... Your ten o'clock appointment has arrived.

DR GRUBER: Yes, show him through

(Exit receptionist ... after a few seconds, enter Moses.)

GRUBER: *(Welcoming his patient)* Hello, Mr ... Mr ... Moses? Is there no surname?

MOSES: My family didn't give me one and the documents don't tell us.

GRUBER: Not to worry ... Take a seat ... So tell me, Mr ... *(Slight pause)* ... Moses. What seems to be the problem?

MOSES: I don't know where to start ... I think I'm ... You'll think I'm stupid or something. You'll ...

GRUBER: Not to worry, Mr Moses. Just take your time and tell me the whole tale. We've got as long as it takes.

MOSES: You don't mind me rabbiting on?

GRUBER: Why should I mind? It's costing you £400 an hour.

MOSES: *(Leaping to his feet)* How much?

GRUBER: You want to be cured, don't you?

MOSES: Well, I'll get straight to the point ... If this is £400, I'm gonna sing like a canary. Last night I was out tending my father-in-law's sheep, when I saw this Angel.

GRUBER: Ah ... An Angel ... Ghostly apparitions.

MOSES: It was shiny and wearing a dress.

GRUBER: These servants of God have always been into cross-dressing. Probably an early David Bowie fan. Pray continue.

MOSES: Then I saw this burning bush.

GRUBER: Ah, a burning bush, you say?

MOSES: Yeah, there was this bush and it was ... *(Pause)* ... burning.

GRUBER: And what is so unusual about that?

MOSES: Well, it wasn't burning.

GRUBER: But you just said it was.

MOSES: I know what I said. It was ... but it wasn't.

GRUBER: Mr Moses, this is costing you £400 an hour, so I'd get the story straight if I were you.

MOSES: It was burning ... but it wasn't.

GRUBER: Mr Moses, I put it to you that you have been drinking.

MOSES: It's not true ... I was stone cold sober. I was tending the sheep and then I saw this bush, which was burning, but it wasn't.

GRUBER: Alright, if you say so. Pray continue, Mr Moses.

MOSES: Then I heard a voice. The voice of God.

GRUBER: Ah, the voice of God. This is all starting to make sense now. Visions and voices. Paranormal activity. What accent was the voice speaking in?

MOSES: What?

GRUBER: What type of voice?

MOSES: Sounded working class to me. South American?

GRUBER: Now, Mr Moses, I must caution you against wasting my time. Don't forget the £400 per hour.

MOSES: I'm not wasting your time.

GRUBER: Mr Moses, would you have us believe that God is a southern, long-haired, Diego Maradona, corned-beef-eating type? I think not!

MOSES: He sounded Argentinian! He could have been a Liberation theologian!

GRUBER: Mr Moses, are you trying to tell me that the Supreme Being, the maker of all that is, seen and unseen, hails from a country that has a tenuous grasp of pluralistic democratic traditions, and cheats at football?

MOSES: Well, I could have been mistaken.

GRUBER: Are you sure the voice was not German? Now, I could believe the Supreme Being was of good Aryan stock. The Germans are so sound and sensible.

MOSES: *(Exasperated)* I don't care where God comes from! All I want to know is whether I'm cracking up or not.

GRUBER: You don't care where God comes from? Mr Moses, this could change the whole history of our existence as we know it. If God turns out to be from Belgium, then the entire universe was created by a cake-eating, European nonentity. If God had a Spanish accent, then that would probably explain why he only worked a six-day week when he was creating the earth. Now, if he was German, well that's OK. But it could be worse – you could be telling me that he's Black! Heaven forbid ... *(Looking at Moses, seeking reassurance)* You're not, are you?

MOSES: *(Exasperated)* I don't care ...

GRUBER: If you insist ... Pray continue, Mr Moses.

MOSES: The voice started to speak to me. It told me to take off my sandals, as I was on holy ground. *(Gruber nods)* The voice told me that I would be the deliverer of the Jews, as I am to be the one to lead them out of Egypt.

GRUBER: Is that so? And how did God instruct you to address him?

MOSES: God said I should use the term, I AM THAT I AM.

GRUBER: Ah, so God is the enigmatic, shy, retiring type … He must be Swiss.

MOSES: That's basically it, Doc … So what do you think?

GRUBER: *(Pulling out a file and flicking through it)* Mr Moses, I have read your case history and, to be frank, looking at your family background, I think there could well be a case for professional treatment.

MOSES: Do you think so?

GRUBER: According to these records, you were abandoned as a child. Social Services messing up again, I see. You were then adopted. Illegally, I might add, by an Egyptian family, without any family checks whatsoever and against strict official practice, which forbids cross-cultural transfers.

MOSES: Cross-cultural transfers?

GRUBER: You are Jewish and your adoptive family were Egyptian. No wonder you're suffering emotional and psychological traumas. Then there's your strained marriage to Zipporah and your ambiguous relationship with your brother Aaron. Then, most seriously of all, you are still wanted for murder. You killed an Egyptian official. Moses, despite my sympathy for your plight and the £400 per hour you are paying me, I still have to hand you in to the authorities. It's for the best.

(Gruber claps his hands and on run two police officers. Moses leaps to his feet and takes Gruber as a hostage.)

MOSES: You'll never take me alive.

GRUBER: Don't be stupid, Mr Moses. You can't escape.

MOSES: We'll see about that. No prison can hold me. And besides, I was doing God's will. I heard the voices, God told me to do it. You will pay for this. God's on my side. I shall set my people free.

(Moses knocks over Gruber, turns and runs off into the distance. The two officers quickly follow him, leaving Gruber alone. Gruber climbs off the floor and begins to dust himself off.)

GRUBER: *(Sarcastically)* Yes, yes, of course he will … *(Slight pause)* What a preposterous thought. Hearing the voice of God? Like God would be Argentinian anyway! God can't possibly be Argentinean. German maybe, but not an Argie. At least he's not Italian. That would be enough to turn me into an Atheist … *(Shakes himself)* What a horrid thought.

THE END

———◄◌►———

Post-sketch reflections

One of the most intriguing aspects of Christianity is the question of 'personal experience'. Normative, classical Christianity claims that an individual can gain a personal experience of God in Christ by means of the Holy Spirit. On the face of it, this claim must seem fantastical to some, yet to others it is an uncontested and irrefutable reality of life. In a previous piece of research I have argued that many older Black people living in the UK have a very personalised and literal appropriation of Jesus in their lives.[3] God in general and Jesus in particular are not simply rationalised concepts but are experiential truths. Jesus becomes the best friend, the fellow struggler in solidarity in the midst of myriad trials and tribulations.[4]

This facet of Christianity is both one of its enduring strengths as well as being a major weakness. In terms of the former, countless men and women have been inspired by the realness and nearness of God in order to create change in their individual lives and in the lives of others.[5] Yet, as James Cone, the 'founding father' of Black Liberation theology, once remarked in an address given at the Queens Foundation in Birmingham in 1997, the most dangerous people in the world are those who claim to have an untrammelled line of communication to God and know exactly what God wants and what can be construed as God's will. In effect, these are the scary people who later claim, 'God told me to do it', when they are arrested for some extreme atrocity.

So what are we to make of this elusive thing called religious experience? Whose experience counts? Who can be trusted to speak for or about God? Scholars such as Jeff Astley[6] and Grant Shockley[7] have questioned the motivation of the hierarchy of the Church in their attempts to limit or even curtail the extent to which ordinary lay people can articulate their own theology. Does the Church trust ordinary lay people to work out and articulate their own theology in the light of their experiences?

On the many occasions when I have used this sketch with groups, I have been struck by the ways in which various individuals have noticed the many value judgements the psychiatrist makes when he is questioning Moses. The psychiatrist, a recognised authority figure, is clear about what God is not like. God, for example, cannot possibly be Argentinean, nor can *he*[8] be Black, but it is not unreasonable to suppose that God might be German. In many respects, as befits a consciously surreal piece of drama, the nationality of God is a fairly ridiculous or facetious question. Clearly, God cannot be identified with any nationality in such a direct way.

And yet, simply look at the reading list of most theology courses or theological libraries, and then note the nationality of the major scholars whose experience and thinking has helped to define theology. Are not the greater preponderance of such scholars Germans? How many of the scholars that populate most theology reading lists are White European males? How many Black people of African origin are in evidence? To what extent have specific African or more generally non-European concepts influenced our theological thinking?[9]

I remember teaching a very experienced ministerial student a number of years ago who had already studied theology at bachelor, masters and doctorate levels, and yet when I mentioned James Cone to him in an introductory lecture to Black theology, this student had never heard of him.

Many of the groups with whom I have worked with this sketch have noticed the scepticism with which Moses is being interrogated by the psychiatrist. Moses is viewed with suspicion, bordering on derision. A number of participants, particularly those who are Black, have recognised in the encounter at the heart of this drama aspects of their own experience. Interviews with a number of Black young people have alerted me to the reluctance of many of them to submit themselves to (predominantly) White authority in terms of 'testing their calling' for ministry (local preaching or ordained ministry).[10] They feel that the truth claims of their calling are always viewed with suspicion, sometimes bordering on derision. Yet, I submit that this kind of scrutiny and scepticism is not levelled at White Oxbridge males!

To what extent are Black and other minority ethnic people believed in their religious experience? Are poor Black and White people trusted? Are they believed? Are their religious experiences and spiritualities given any veracity? What criteria are used to determine the truth of any God-talk?[11]

Follow-up questions

Read selected parts of the Book of Exodus, focusing on chapters 2–13 (Moses' early life). Having reflected on the sketch, consider the following questions:

- Moses claims to have heard voices and seen a burning bush. If you have felt called by or have experienced God, did you tell anyone? If yes, then what did you say? If no, then why not?
- The African American comedian Bill Cosby once remarked that only stupid people see Martians, because smart people know better than to tell others about it. Do you think the same is true about experiencing God in a dramatic or mysterious way? Who shares their stories and who does not?
- Moses is not from an important or influential family, and yet God calls him directly and uses him for the liberation of Israel. Who are the people most likely to be called by God in our present age? Are there some people more likely to be called than others, and if so, who are they?
- To what extent are some people believed more than others when they share their experiences and talk about the truth?
- What kind of factors influence who is heard and the seriousness with which we hear them?

A Run of Bad Luck

Opening reflections

One of the most troubling questions that confronts theologians and so-called ordinary Christians alike has been the explanation for the existence of pain, struggle and death. If God is all powerful, whose very essence is love, then why does that same God allow terrible things to happen? I am not going to pretend that I am in possession of any better answers than those constructed by the many thinkers who have wrestled with this issue since the earliest days of the Church's existence. Whilst I cannot supply any easy answers, we need, nonetheless, to wrestle with this issue. So what are we to make of suffering?

I have chosen to address this question by way of writing a short piece about Job. The story of Job presents us with a number of very real problems. In the story of Job, God appears to be very capricious – whimsical and apparently unconcerned about Job's welfare. God appears to use Job and the suffering he endures as the basis for winning a wager against the arch-enemy – Satan. Can this really be the action of an all-loving and caring God? Charles Melchert has offered some interesting reflections on how we can read Job's experiences, and has put them to use in an educational setting.[1]

In the sketch I wanted to highlight Job's descent from comfortable and contented, to despairing and, in my version, at least, almost mentally unwell. (Sorry – artistic licence!)

One of the ways in which Black and marginalised peoples have often been tempted to deal with major issues of suffering and death is to seek identification and solace in the death and resurrection of Jesus. The logic goes something like this: If God allowed Jesus, his very own Son, to die, not sparing him the agonies of the cross, we should not expect God to spare us. But given the way in which Jesus' death leads to resurrection and new life for all humanity (the triumph of the cross), then might not our suffering and death be the gateway to new life and the ultimate reward of being transformed beings in Christ? It is a powerful and seductive argument. Writers such as James Cone[2] and Jacquelyn Grant[3] have seen suffering and death as within the overall scope of God's redemptive plans for humankind – that is, God might not necessarily purposefully send suffering and death onto his people,[4] but he is, however, in the business of transforming these troubling elements in human experience.

Other scholars, most notably William Jones,[5] and more recently Anthony Pinn,[6] have argued that suffering and death can never be redemptive. No form of transformation, learning and resulting new experiences can ever atone for or make the painful experience less than it was, or make it alright or acceptable.

Whichever side of the divide you stand on, we need to try and make sense of this. Looking at the sketch, Job is comfortable. He has a good life. He owns property and people, and is rightly proud of his family. It would appear that he has begun to measure his success and progress in terms of the possessions he has amassed and the good standing in which he is held by his peers.

The notable 'dub'[7] poet Linton 'Kwesi' Johnson has argued that the progressive struggle of Black peoples in Britain since the 'Empire Windrush' in 1948 has been dulled by our acquisition of consumer gifts and social advancement.[8] In a similar vein, Harold Dean Trulear argues that the radicalism of the Black Church in the USA has been blunted by the rise of classism and the dominance of middle-class values and aspirations.[9]

Previous generations of Christian believers seemed able to deal with hardship, pain and death by locating the source of all things (whether good or not so good) in God.[10] In our more sceptical and, dare one say, postmodern times, does the same resilience exist within people who claim to be followers of Christ?

Whilst many societies in the West have grown and developed, becoming more technologically sophisticated, the lot of the poor and the marginalised remains not only the same, but in many respects, it has grown worse. How do these people make sense of pain, suffering and death? Can they claim the same sense of redemptive victory over the dark forces of oppression as did their ancestors? Is it sufficient to say that God is in control, or do we need more? Consider these points as you perform the following sketch.

———◄◦►———

A Run of Bad Luck

(We see a solitary man standing on stage. This is Job.)

JOB: People say to me, 'Job, why do you believe in God? I mean, what has God ever done for you?' And do you know what I say to them? I say, 'Friend, trust in Jehovah. He is a God who knows how to look after his own.' Take me, for instance. Look what he's done for me … God has given me everything. I'm one lucky guy. I've got a devilishly saucy-looking wife, who's a bit of alright, if you get my drift. A gorgeous-looking daughter who has all the men in the neighbourhood running around like frisky dogs. Three strapping sons who can beat any man to death who so much as throws one indecent look at my daughter. A huge palatial mansion, a tribe of servants who all love me, a truck-load of original oxen, a dumper-truck full of sexy-looking sheep, a herd of delicious donkeys and most amazingly of all, a couple of curvaceous camels … My, how I love my camels … I just love camels. And if all this weren't enough, I'm also blessed with the most magnificent hunky good looks. Mine are the kind of looks grown men kill for … *(Begins to admire himself)* Dig that smooth-looking skin, the deep, rich tan and rugged good looks. Yep, I hate to say it, but I am one awesome-looking guy … And God has given me all this. So I don't want to hear anyone dissing my God again … You dig?

(Enter a messenger, running frantically, who approaches Job.)

MESSENGER 1: Mr Job … I'm afraid I've got some bad news … I'd hmm … I'd take a seat, if I were you, Sir … You're not going to like this.

JOB: Come, come now, servant, it can't possibly be that bad. Speak up man, out with it.

MESSENGER 1: Well …

JOB: Come on, speak up.

MESSENGER 1: Well, Sir … There was a party at the family house yesterday, when you were away on business. While the party was taking place, the Sabeans attacked and carried off all your oxen and donkeys. They also killed your servants. Only I escaped … Sorry, Sir.

(Exit Messenger 1.)

JOB: Oh, well … I guess it's for the best. After all, they're only dumb animals, and, as for the servants, you can buy them anywhere … I can live with this … No problem. I'm a man … I can take this kind of rejection. I've got a strong, manly, handsome chin.

(Enter another messenger.)

MESSENGER 2: *(Shouting)* FIRE! FIRE! Fire, fire everywhere, and not a drop to drink!

JOB: *(Trying to calm down the messenger)* Not a drop to drink?

MESSENGER 2: Oh, sorry, Sir … I was over-acting. We bit players are always doing it. It's the ego, you know.

JOB: OK, OK, get on with the message … What's this fire you're babbling on about?

MESSENGER 2: Whilst I was working in the fields, I suddenly saw a huge bolt of lightning, which came down from the sky and set fire to all your sheep and the servants tending them … I was the only one who survived.

JOB: Fire from the sky?

MESSENGER 2: Just like in a bad Hollywood movie starring Charlton Heston.

JOB: All my sheep?

MESSENGER 2: Every last one, Sir.

JOB: How badly burnt were the sheep?

MESSENGER 2: I hope you don't like your meat rare, Sir.

JOB: *(Stunned)* All my sheep? … But … what am I going to do now?

MESSENGER 2: Hold a barbeque? You've got enough meat to go round, particularly if you like mutton … *(Pause)* Charcoal style.

JOB: This is … This is …

MESSENGER 2: What about the servants, Sir?

JOB: *(Angry)* Sod the servants! Who cares about the servants? Useless, dumb servants. Dumb, stupid underlings. But my sheep. God, what are you playing at?

(Whilst this is going on, re-enter Messenger 1.)

MESSENGER 1: Woe is me … Woe, woe and thrice woe. Woe is me … Titter ye not, Madam. Nay, I say. Not on ye nellie, Madam.

JOB & MESSENGER 2: What?

MESSENGER 1: *(Embarrassed)* Hmmm ... Sorry. I was over-acting too. You don't like Frankie Howerd?

JOB: Get on with it. What's with all this 'Woe is me' nonsense?

MESSENGER 1: More bad news, Sir. I think you'd better take a seat, 'cos it's not good.

JOB: To the point!

MESSENGER 1: The Chaldeans formed a raiding party and swept down on your camels and carried them both off.

JOB: *(Incredulous)* My camels?

MESSENGER 1: The two curvaceous ones.

JOB: Betsy and Snugglebun?

MESSENGER 1: Betsy and Snugglebun ... He was crying as he was leaving.

JOB: Who, Snugglebun?

MESSENGER 1: No, one of the men from the raiding party. Betsy stood on his toe.

(Job falls to the floor and begins to sob hysterically.)

JOB: Well, thanks a lot, God. Thank you for everything. This is just brilliant. I don't mind losing the donkeys, the servants and the sheep ... But Betsy and Snugglebun? God, have you no compassion? At least things can't get much worse.

(A figure at the side of the stage motions to Messenger 2, who runs across and collects a slip of paper and returns to Job and Messenger 1.)

MESSENGER 2: *(Looking at the bit of paper in his hand)* About things not getting much worse ...

JOB: *(Sitting down)* I know the drill. Get to the point.

MESSENGER 2: I've just received a message, Sir ... Your sons and daughters were having a party, an *agape* love feast in memory of Betsy and Snugglebun, when suddenly a mighty wind swept in from the desert and struck the house at all corners. It collapsed and they are all dead. Only one servant escaped.

JOB: *(Slowly getting to his feet)* Great! Absolutely fantastic! Remarkable! Now I lose my entire family ... I'll miss those camels, though.

MESSENGER 2: Sir, can we help?

JOB: *(Turning on the messengers)* No, you cannot. Now get out, both of you.

(Exit both messengers.)

JOB: So much for my happiness, huh? What else can possibly go wrong?

(On runs another messenger. Without saying a word, the messenger begins to place small bits of Blu-tack all over Job's face and arms. Job looks on silently.)

JOB: *(Looking at the messenger)* What are you doing?

MESSENGER 3: You've been cursed … You've got boils, bumps, pimples and mega-huge zits of mountainous proportions … Have a nice day.

(Exit Messenger 3. Job is standing alone, motionless. After a few seconds we see a salesperson walking across the stage.)

SALESPERSON: *(Shouting out)* Topex … Get your Topex here. Lovely Topex. Burn that skin, napalm those zits … *(Stops and looks at Job)* Say, buddy, you're a mighty spotty person. I could play join-the-dots on your face. Do you want me to do you a huge favour?

JOB: Leave me alone …

(Exit Salesperson.)

JOB: *(Arms aloft)* Isn't life wonderful? I'm so happy. *(Begins to laugh hysterically)* … I'm so happy, happy, happy happy. I'm so very happy.

(Enter two psychiatric nurses in white jackets. They both get a hold of Job's arms and begin to walk him off stage.)

JOB: *(Mumbling incoherently to himself)* Happy happy happy happy. I'm so very happy.

NURSE: We apologise for this, but Mr Job isn't feeling well. We'll be seeing you later. He'll be back when the drugs kick in and the treatments begin to work. Sorry about this. Frightfully embarrassing, but what can you do when the leading man goes cuckoo? … Sorry about that. Bye.

THE END

Post-sketch reflections

This sketch has been one of the most challenging for me on a personal level. Since my late teens I have struggled with the notion of suffering as having any special or redemptive qualities. Having witnessed at first hand the struggles of many Black people living in the Caribbean, I have wondered about the seemingly pernicious ways in which the Christian faith has sought to spiritualise the realities of suffering. I have been suspicious of the ways in which Christian tradition through the Church has attempted to almost make a virtue of suffering, likening human suffering to Christ's ordeal on the cross.[11] Often, it is the people who have the least personal or experiential understanding of suffering who want to make it a theological virtue.

Having used this sketch with a number of groups, I have been intrigued at how various individuals have responded to Job's plight. I think it is fair to say that there has been no general consensus in how people have attempted to make sense of Job's plight in particular and suffering in general. For some, suffering is entirely consistent with God's nature. The cross lies at the heart of God's redemptive plans for humankind. Jesus' own injunction to his potential followers to take up their cross and follow him,[12] seems to suggest that suffering is an important ingredient of Christian discipleship, if not the human condition. Conversely, others have stated that to suggest that God's plan for humanity wills and intends suffering is to identify God as a sadist.

Whilst there has been no general consensus in how people have responded to the sketch, I have noted an interesting dichotomy in the responses that have emerged in workshops. The split can be divided into two categories. In the first camp are those who might be described as the 'accepters'. By 'accepters', I mean those who can seem to accept the notion of suffering: whilst it may not come from God or be sanctioned by God, it can be redemptive. A number of these 'accepters' tended to be older individuals from poorer socio-economic backgrounds, in which poverty and hardship are real factors in their lived experience.

The many conversations that arose from the accounts of the 'accepters' around their experiences of growth and transformation from suffering have led me to ponder on whether such certainty was a measure of their immense depth of faith or is reflective of a real sense of psychological denial. To what extent were these individuals certain of God's redemptive work through suffering, or was this certainty a symptom of the need to find some emotional or psychological comfort to deal with the unremitting pain and hardship of life?[13] It is beyond the scope of this book to make any assessment on this query, but it is a question that continues to exercise my grey matter.

Alongside the 'accepters' are the 'discontents'. The latter tend to be younger, with more formal education and greater life opportunities than the former. Unlike the 'accepters', the 'discontents' remain steadfastly unconvinced about the redemptive powers of suffering. In terms of this latter group, I have often wondered whether the relative material success of these individuals (as compared to the 'accepters') has made them less able to deal with the harshness of suffering. It is interesting to note the relative differences between older Black theologians such as James Cone[14] and J. Deotis Roberts,[15] and younger scholars such as Anthony Pinn[16] and Victor Anderson.[17] The former lived through the brunt of the pre-civil rights era when the realities of lynchings in the American South were still very much a part of the cultural and social landscape. Conversely, their younger counterparts do not have that same direct experience of or relationship to struggle. To what extent have the relative progress and advantages accrued by a younger generation of people given them the space and ease to intellectualise on the merits or otherwise of divine solidarity in and through suffering, compared to the more literal appropriation of God's providence in their older counterparts? Am I (as a tentative member of the 'discontents') guilty of using the relative improvements in my own experience as an opportunity to indulge in postmodern doubting when compared to my parents' generation?

Follow-up questions

Read selected parts of chapters 2, 3, 4, 6, 10, 12, 13, 16, 19 and 21 from the Book of Job. Having considered Job's predicament from both the Bible and the sketch, consider the following:

- How would we react to hardship and such a run of bad luck?
- What events or losses would tip you 'over the edge'?
- What is the worst thing that has ever happened to you or to someone you know?
- In times of severe hardship, suffering or pain, have you prayed to God to 'put things right'? If yes, what did you expect God to do? What happened?
- Do you believe in 'happy ever after' endings (resurrection, for example)? Why or why not?

- Does the 'happy ending' make the suffering and struggle acceptable?
- Can suffering and death be redeemed or made better?
- If it could be proved that suffering and death are part of life but have no intrinsic meaning or explanation, then what would we make of God?

Psalm 23: A Modern Version for 21st-Century Sceptics

Opening reflections

One of my earliest memories of growing up in a Jamaican household in Bradford was of my mother preparing a meal in the kitchen whilst reciting Psalm 23. My mother knew the psalm intimately and recited it with great clarity and without the need of a book. I suspect that she, along with many of her peers, could not only recite it from memory, but also believed implicitly in its sentiments and theological truths. I have highlighted something to this effect in a previous book.[1]

I am aware that in the one generation between my mother and myself there already exists a marked difference in our respective spiritualities. I am, perhaps, less trusting and convinced of God's providence than my mother. Perhaps she needed to believe in God's undoubted goodness more than I do. (See the previous piece on Job and the post-sketch reflections.) Given these differences, then what are we to make of a younger generation that is perhaps even more sceptical, consumerist and materialistic than my own?

A number of biblical commentaries suggest that this psalm became an important part of the liturgy of the early Church, particularly around the sacraments, such as Baptism and Holy Communion. The psalmist speaks of an enduring trust and dependence upon God, one which responds to the many changes and challenges of life. Although this psalm was written long before Jesus' earthly ministry, the inclusion of the term 'shepherd' soon became synonymous with Jesus himself. Jesus, after all, described himself as the 'Good Shepherd' (John 10:11).

Throughout the psalm there is a relationship between the grace and goodness of God and the authority and lordship of God over the life of the writer. It is as if there is a reciprocal agreement between the two. God offers security and care, but expects obedience and service. Themes that still speak to us today in our Christian discipleship.

So what of a younger generation, or even those not so young? Where do our security and expectations lie? In God? In material success? In the expected rewards of life? Whereas older generations of marginalised and poor people were seemingly able to aspire for greater rewards in life, their sense of identity and security was often located in God, and God's goodness.[2] In our present age, despite the continuing search by many young adults and teenagers for a viable spirituality,[3] we none-theless are faced with a deeply materialistic culture that often por-trays the market and consumerism as king. We seem to live in a world where the material matters more than the spiritual, where lifestyle and individuality are more important than service and community.

In response to many of these issues, and as a challenge to my own self, I wrote the following dialogue. It is a deeply cynical reading of Psalm 23. Perhaps I have overstated the case in writing this piece. See what you think. Compare and contrast the two voices. Where do you stand? One is a deeply spiritual and theological response to God. The other is a materialistically self-driven ideal of life, with God thrown in from time to time as a form of justification.

———◄○►———

Psalm 23: A Modern Version for 21st-Century Sceptics

(A dramatic reading for two people. Voice No. 1 is a woman and Voice No. 2 is a man.)

NO. 1: The Lord is my shepherd. I shall not be in want.

NO. 2: The Lord is my Shepherd. He gives me everything I want. Gucci shoes, leather jackets, Nike trainers, Levi jeans, Rayban glasses, Ben Sherman shirts and a whole host of postmodernist consumer-type leisure-wear.

NO. 1: He makes me lie down in green pastures.

NO. 2: I don't know about that, but I was at my stag party last week when some of my so-called friends grabbed me by the scruff of the neck and pulled me through some very long grass … Which was wet, by the way. Then they chained me to a metal pole. They said that I should do penance for all the sins committed in my bachelor days. And God did nothing to stop them. Well, thanks a lot, God. What did

I ever do to you? I know they're a set of no-good low-lives, but I expected better of you. Hit me right where it hurts, why don't you?

NO. 1: He leads me besides quiet waters, he restores my soul.

NO. 2: Having punished me in the long grass, God then led me away for a quiet retreat to the Lake District for a bit of solitude and peace. He thought I took my punishment from my friends like a man and didn't whimper and cry … Well, not much. We went to Lake Coniston, the bit close to the ice-cream van, just to the left of the pub. We didn't go in, honest … Oh, and he restores my soul as well. Whatever!

NO. 1: He guides me in paths of righteousness for his sake.

NO. 2: *(Looking perplexed)* What does that mean? Paths of righteousness? Sorry, but it doesn't mean diddly to me. Was the path of righteousness the one next to the pond in Regents Park?

NO. 1: Even though I walk through the Valley of the Shadow of Death, I will fear no evil, for you are with me.

NO. 2: Are you kidding? Have you seen that valley? It's all dark and spooky-looking in there. Those shadows are big and some mean-looking gangs hang out in that place. Only last week I was walking through that valley, when I was jumped by three bikers. The type of guys who need some severe spiritual counselling. The type you administer with a big stick. Well, these guys beat the crap out of me. 'I will fear no evil'? Not in this lifetime, buddy-boy. Are you for real? What kind of wacko are you?

NO. 1: Your rod and your staff, they comfort me.

NO. 2: Because of my mugging in the Valley of the Shadow of Death, I bought me a rod and staff to protect myself. And my, did it comfort me? You betcha! It was very comforting. The next time those guys came around, I showed them a thing or two. I used the rod and the staff and it was extremely effective, and my, was I comforted. All the way to a police cell for grievous bodily harm. What kind of world is it, that a man can get arrested for simply defending himself? The system is crazy, guy.

NO. 1: You prepare a table before me in the presence of my enemies.

NO. 2: Whilst I was in the clink, my intended brought me some food to keep me going. Their canteen food tastes like it was cooked in raw sewage. I had chicken drumsticks, caviar, prawns, smoked salmon, even some back-of-the-market hotdogs. Yummy!

NO. 1: You anoint my head with oil; my cup overflows.

NO. 2: My partner hatched a cunning plan to get me out of the cell. She brought me some stinky scent whilst I was in the clink. Was I a popular cell-mate with the rest of the detainees? I poured it all over my head and I stank the place out completely. They threw me out of the station pretty sharpish. We celebrated with a mug of champagne. My cup did overflow … Many, many times. You should have seen me. I got so drunk, I dropped my trousers and …

NO. 1: *(Hastily interrupting No. 2)* Surely goodness and love will follow me all the days of my life.

NO. 2: My partner forgave me for my little drunken indiscretion last night. I offered her a cheap ring from the local market and she promised to love me for the rest of my days, so long as I make enough money to continue paying her. Partners don't come cheap anymore.

NO. 1: And I will dwell in the house of the Lord for ever.

NO. 2: Yep, I can't argue with that … God is certainly good. I've done my bit for charity, so I think I deserve it. He's even preparing a room for me right at this very moment, in his celestial home in heaven. I used to share a bedroom with my younger brother when I was younger. We shared a bed, which he used to wet nearly every night. So you can see I can't wait to go to heaven and get that room all to myself. After all, that's what it's all about, isn't it? Doing your bit, trusting in God? Saying all the right stuff! Getting your reward! It's worth it in the end. I'm right religious, I am. Can't get enough of the stuff.

NO. 1: Amen.

NO. 2: Amen.

THE END

———◄◦►———

Post-sketch reflections

I am often accused by some of my friends of being much too cynical for my own good, and to some extent they have a point. I am, on a number of occasions, guilty of thinking or assuming the worst, but I usually counter such charges by simply pointing to the evidence – the world gives me much cause to assume the worst. The response from groups who have worked with this dialogue has been mixed. For some, it is much too critical and cynical. The voice of No. 2 is not one they recognise. Whilst it is not the purpose of this book to instruct or guide individuals into particular ways of thinking, I have challenged those individuals who have responded negatively to the attitude of No. 2 to reflect more critically on their own lives. To what extent does the relative politeness and reasonableness of much church life in the UK (overwhelmingly White and middle class) simply mask the explicit selfishness that is exhibited by character No. 2 in the dialogue?

Many Christians may use the language of 'doing God's will' or 'denying self in order to follow Christ'.[4] In my more cynical moments (taking my own life and commitments as an initial starting point), I have wondered whether the noble words of such declarations are nothing more than mere romantic rhetoric. Whilst we would all like to believe that we are in the business of putting Christ first and denying ourselves, the truth is, there is precious little evidence of such commitment within the capitalistic societies of the West. The renowned Sri Lankan theologian, Tissa Balasuriya, has argued for the need to develop a theology for the affluent – one that will challenge the tendency of comfortable Christians in the West to indulge in wholesale, collective actions of 'cheap grace' when confronted with the radicalism and potency of the Gospel.[5]

What are the links, I wonder, between the manifestly selfish and narcissistic individual in the dialogue and the many Christians who steadfastly refuse to pay higher taxes so that the underclass can be given even the faintest stake in many of our affluent Western societies? Is not character No. 2 simply being honest about his or her motivation and expectations?

Conversely, there are others who have argued that character No. 2 is really many of us without the polite veneer or façade of forced piety.[6] I have been pleasantly surprised at the number of people who have recognised the many ways in which we all collude with the blandishments of materialism and consumerism, and then give token amounts of money to charity in order to salve our consciences and justify our lifestyles in response to the claims of the Gospel. Scholars such as Ann-Cathrin Jarl have attempted to remind Christian communities, particularly those in the West, of the ethical claims of the Gospel.[7]

There are increasing numbers of people who are very much committed to being in solidarity with those who are the most vulnerable and in need, in many of the rich nations in the West, and also with those from the so-called 'developing nations'. Organisations such as Christian Aid, Traidcraft and Cafod have been active in making people critically aware of the implications of Christian faith on their lifestyles and commitments.

Clearly, it does not take a rocket scientist to perceive the ideological or political subtext that lies beneath the surface of these debates or discussions. This point is addressed more explicitly in a later piece in this book.[8] The debates surrounding this dialogue have tended to divide broadly along a 'left' versus 'right' axis in terms of political and cultural commitment and awareness. For some, character No. 2 is not representative of any wider structural or systemic concerns – that is, he or she is not some crude archetype. Rather, he/she is simply an example of a selfish approach to religious faith. His/her actions are in no way linked to the collective failures or attitudes that affect all of us, including those who have observed or performed the dialogue.

Alternatively, there are others who would say exactly the opposite – that the crude depiction of this individual is very much the dark, narcissistic alter ego of many aspirational Christians, and as such, is an archetype of a structural and systemic fault-line in Western Christianity. What do you think?

Follow-up questions

Re-read Psalm 23 and the dialogue once again. Consider the following questions:

- If someone asked who or what was the supreme guiding presence in your life, what would be your answer? (And why?)
- Assuming that many of you might say God or Jesus, how would you demonstrate the reality of this fact to another person who did not know God or Jesus?
- Many Christians will claim that they only aspire to do God's will. Looking at your lifestyle – your time commitments, hobbies, the way you earn and spend money – what would you say might be the

alternatives that motivate you or the desires that drive you?

- If, on a line from 1 to 20, voice No. 1 in the sketch is represented at 20 and voice No. 2 is at 1, then where would you place yourself in terms of your response to God? Why would you place yourself at this position?
- What things would you need to change in your life in order to push yourself up the scale towards 20?
- What part should 'contentment' and 'acceptance' play in our Christian discipleship?
- What should we be content and satisfied with? When is it right not to be content or satisfied?

Complaints

Opening reflections

In a world of conformity and alleged normality, we can all think of people who, as the saying goes, 'stick out like a sore thumb'. The people who are so different, either in terms of dress, attitude, behaviour or beliefs, that they challenge the rest of us, and if truth be told, make us feel very uncomfortable.

I went to a large comprehensive school on the outskirts of Bradford called Tong Upper School. Of all the people who attended that school, the one who had the greatest impact upon me was my history teacher. He stood out like a sore thumb. He communicated with young people in a natural and cringe-free way. It might be over-stating matters to call him a prophet, but I am sure that countless young people owe him a great debt for the way in which he inspired us.

It has often been said that hindsight is 'twenty-twenty vision'. We can all see in hindsight who the great prophets and visionaries of our age have been. So Nelson Mandela is revered by the whole world, even the political right, who once dubbed him a criminal. There was a time when one could not mention Nelson Mandela without remarking upon his then amazing companion, Winnie. Now Winnie is no longer in vogue, I wonder what time and posterity will make of her? We now have Martin Luther King as a latter-day saint, even amongst conservative southerners in the US, but he was abused and disparaged during his own lifetime.

One of the popular slogans that emerges at Black conferences and educational events is: 'Not his-story, but true history'.[1] What the slogan is attempting to articulate is the biased, selective way in which history has been constructed – one in which the achievements of Black people and people of colour are erased in favour of European-inspired events and ideals. This is no less true in terms of how we understand and relate to the Bible and Christianity as a whole. Black biblical scholars such as Randall Bailey,[2] Gay Byron[3] and Cain Hope Felder[4] have argued for the need to rediscover a Black presence within biblical and early Christian literature.

The experience of poor, marginalised and oppressed peoples within Christian history and the Church has largely been one of struggle, opposition and invisibility. We have often been perceived as problems rather than opportunities. We have been controlled, denigrated and treated with suspicion. Only in recent history has our presence within White-majority churches been celebrated.[5]

In the life, actions and witness of John the Baptist we see someone who was undoubtedly viewed with hostility and suspicion by the political and religious establishment of his time. He was seen as a disturbing presence. A difficult and troublesome customer who would no more play by the biased, self-serving rules of his day than did the likes of Mary Prince,[6] Olaudah Equiano[7] and Ignatius Sancho.[8] These individuals, all Black slaves who resided at some point in their lives in London, were key figures in the abolition movement, and yet for the most part have been written out of history.

British Methodism has quite rightly made much of its radical past, particularly the links with and the empowerment of Black and other working-class people. John Wesley was an ardent opponent of the Atlantic slave trade. Yet, I would argue that the most vociferous voice against slavery came not from the established voices of eighteenth-century Methodism, as documented in the official histories, but rather from the often hidden presence of the likes of Sancho and Ottabah Cugoano.[9]

So what are we to make of John the Baptist? Why was he so threatening to the ruling elite of his time? How do we relate to him and to others like him? Consider some of these thoughts as you perform the following sketch.

————◄◦►————

Complaints

(The scene is a police station. We see a Police Captain pacing the floor. A telephone rings. He runs to the phone and answers it.)

POLICE CAPTAIN: *(New York accent)* Yes, Captain Dartelli here. What? Who? I'm sorry. I can't make out a word you're saying. Who? Ah ... John the Baptist ... Sorry, don't know him. Why is he called that? ... *(Slight pause)* ... He baptises people? Why does he do that? Can't they take baths for themselves? Oh, I see. It's a religious thing. Well, don't talk to me about it. See a priest or something. It's not my problem.

(Slams down the telephone ... begins to pace the room for a few more seconds, when the telephone rings again. He answers it.)

CAPTAIN: Yes, Captain Dartelli ... What? Not this Baptist again. What is wrong with this guy? Can't he get a proper job, instead of going around throwing smelly people into rivers and bathing them? Look, Doberman, I don't need this hassle, I really don't ... These Baptists, they're the worst. It's always the Baptists who insist on going around giving people baths. You never catch the Methodists doing that kind of thing. The Anglicans can't be bothered, and as for most Catholics – well, let's say that water isn't their thing, if you get my drift ... What's that? You don't get that reference? Well, I'm not explaining it. All I'm saying is, the Catholics don't cause so much botheration like these damn Baptists. What's the joker's name again? John the Baptist. No, what's his real name? ... *(Slight pause)* ... I know he's called John. What's his surname? Look, Doberman, don't mess me about. I know his surname isn't Baptist. You're not telling me there is a family running around Judea with Baptist as a surname. Don't tell me, his father is called 'I-was-born-a' and his mother goes by the name of 'Used-to-be-a' ... No, Doberman, don't write that down, it was a joke. A bad one, I know, but I was trying to be humorous. Idiot. Look, keep me posted. OK?

(Slams down the telephone again. At that moment, enter a Junior Officer. He approaches the Captain.)

JUNIOR OFFICER: *(Nervous)* Hmmm, Sir.

CAPTAIN: What is it?

JUNIOR OFFICER: We've got a public disturbance on our hands.

CAPTAIN: Who is involved?

JUNIOR OFFICER: Some strange man wearing camel hair and a thick leather belt.

CAPTAIN: A weirdo, then.

JUNIOR OFFICER: He has very long hair.

CAPTAIN: So he's a weirdo traveller.

JUNIOR OFFICER: He eats locusts and wild honey.

CAPTAIN: A weirdo traveller with bad taste.

JUNIOR OFFICER: He keeps throwing people in the Sea of Galilee.

CAPTAIN: A weirdo traveller, with bad taste and a bathing fetish.

JUNIOR OFFICER: He keeps on slagging off the religious authorities. Calls them hypocrites.

CAPTAIN: A weirdo traveller with bad taste and a bathing fetish, who doubles as an anarchist in his spare time … What's his name?

JUNIOR OFFICER: John the Baptist.

CAPTAIN: *(Exploding)* Give me strength! … What is wrong with this guy? Why can't he behave himself? You can't just go around bathing people in public rivers, wearing Oxfam cast-offs and slagging off the government, and expect people to take you seriously. Who does he think he is? A left-wing Oxbridge drop-out? Look, round up a few men and bring this Baptist joker in for questioning.

JUNIOR OFFICER: But he's very popular, Sir. His fans won't like it.

CAPTAIN: I don't care what his fans say. He's probably just a flash in the pan anyway. Wait 'til his sermons stop selling and people get sick of his dress sense. Don't forget Adam and the Ants … *(Pointing at the Junior Officer)* I want him brought in now.

JUNIOR OFFICER: If you're sure, Sir.

CAPTAIN: Yes, I'm sure … Now bring him in.

(Exit the Junior Officer … The Captain begins to pace the room again. The telephone rings once more.)

CAPTAIN: Captain Dartelli … What have I done to deserve this? What has this locust-and-honey-eating, camel-haired, leather-belt-clad, left-wing, weirdo anarchist done now? … Slagged off King Herod. Well, he's gone too far this time. Bring him in at all costs. I don't care how you do it, just bring him in. Slap him around a bit … Who cares? Say he slipped on a bar of soap – they always believe that one. Just get that looney-tune off the streets and pronto … *(Slams down the telephone)* … Weirdos, don't you just hate them?

(Enter Junior Officer.)

JUNIOR OFFICER: Sir … Do you still want tickets for the Simon and the Mystic Soothsayers concert this evening?

CAPTAIN: *(Exploding)* Get out!

JUNIOR OFFICER: I was only asking.

CAPTAIN: Why is my life plagued by weirdos and self-seeking wannabees? Why can't everyone just play by the rules, behave themselves and know their place? The last thing we need is yet more troublemakers who think they can change the world. As for this Baptist bloke, he won't be bathing any more smelly people when I've finished with him. Jokers!

THE END

———◄○►———

Post-sketch reflections

Writing this sketch was something of a love-hate process. Occasionally, when I am writing a script, I find myself torn between my own individual emotions and the inadvertent course my script is taking. The truth is, as I was writing this piece, I wanted desperately to dislike the police captain. Captain Dartelli is a nasty piece of work. A recent trip to South Africa and witnessing the vicious echoes of the apartheid regime has only brought home the realities of the likes of Dartelli even more chillingly. But the truth is, as one who is often suspicious and cynical about the sometimes exhibitionist tendencies of so-called mavericks,[10] I have to admit to having a secret regard for Dartelli in this sketch.

On the occasions I have used this sketch with different groups, it has been interesting to note the various levels of sympathy for Dartelli. For some, Dartelli is simply a nasty piece of work, whose officious manner simply reminds us of the repressive nature of illegitimate authority. Yet on other occasions, there have been those who, whilst not siding with Dartelli and his ilk, have been sufficiently honest to acknowledge their dislike of 'troublemakers'.

My work with many poor and marginalised groups has reminded me of the inherent conservatism in many of these communities. The radicalism of many so-called iconoclasts, often working on behalf of or with poor and oppressed communities, often goes without appreciation or gratitude from the very groups who are in theory the beneficiaries of such actions. Why should that be the case? Might it be due to the embarrassment some of these groups or communities feel when they sense that particular individuals (especially if they are from their own ranks) are drawing unwarranted attention towards them? Might it not be the sense of wanting to 'keep one's head down' that prevents some communities from supporting mavericks or troublemakers?

It has been interesting to note the number of individuals who, when juxtaposing John the Baptist's actions with those of some contemporary figures, have begun to read into the sketch a sense of collaboration or lack of support for this radical figure. Did anyone within the colonised community of Judea 'give up' John the Baptist? Was he the victim of collaborators?

I have often been intrigued at the ways in which the modern Church has often fallen in love with the rhetoric of prophetic action. From our vantage point of some 2000 years of history, particularly given the fact that we know the 'ending of the story', we often delude ourselves into believing that we welcome the kind of prophetic proclamation (*kerygma*) exemplified by John the Baptist. The truth is, given the reluctance of the institutional Church to embrace radical action,[11] we like to bask in the unearned glory of radical action in hindsight. The groups with whom I have used this sketch have, after prolonged thought and reflection, speculated on the extent to which 'we' would have found John the Baptist a difficult and irritating customer. Might it not be the case that many of us really have more in common with Captain Dartelli than we do with John the Baptist? I am sure that none of us would ever want to consciously acknowledge our culpability in such matters, but given my commitment to critical Christianity, which necessitates a radical re-reading of history, I am suspicious of the unwarranted claims the Church often makes for itself.

Follow-up questions

Read Matthew 3; Mark 6:14–29; Luke 7:18–32.

- Have you ever felt as if you were a troublemaker, or been made to feel like an outsider? Why was that, and how did it feel?
- Have you met or known others who might be considered troublemakers? How did you feel about them? How did you treat them and react to them?
- Why is John the Baptist considered a threat?
- Who are the prophets and subversive people of our age?

- Who have been the challenging voices that have inspired you? Why is that?
- What are the issues and challenges that require a John the Baptist for our present age?
- If you knew someone who had a burning issue on their heart and in their mind, and they came to you for advice regarding what they should do, what advice would you give them?

It Could Have Happened Like This

Opening reflections

The title of this piece is clearly a blatant untruth. The story of Paul's encounter with Eutychus (Acts 20:7–11) clearly did not go like this, as neither person was Jamaican, for a start! But I think you can understand what I'm getting at. This is another example of re-setting a biblical story or narrative in an alternative setting and embedding it in that particular cultural environment – an example of re-contextualisation and inculturation.

A number of scholars have written extensively about Black family life, and the social and cultural factors that affect Black families and their structure.[1] One of the hidden factors of Black life and the cultures that reflect these experiences is the sometimes negative aspects that exist within Black communities and are often overlooked or even excused. I shall deal this with issue in more detail in one of the later sketches.[2]

One such hidden issue is the sense of rivalry, competition and conformity that exists within many Black communities. Oftentimes, Black communities can be harder on themselves than on the external factors that have historically oppressed and limited them.[3] There are many Black people who have been accused of not 'really being Black' or not being 'Black enough'.[4] Writers such as Victor Anderson have challenged the way in which other Black scholars have perpetuated aspects of this internal conformity by refusing to acknowledge the inherent diversity within Black cultural life in the African Diaspora.[5]

One of the issues I wanted to address in the following piece is the question of intra-communal jealousies – the sense that within oppressed and marginalised groups, where racism and poverty are amongst the main factors that define the nature of community, it is often the case that petty rivalries and jealousies are clearly in evidence. To dare to be different or to be seen as different offers a dangerous challenge to the whole community and their notions of what is permissible or acceptable. To be different is to potentially bring shame upon the whole family or community. Shame is a very strong factor in defining the limits on behaviour, identity and action within many Diasporan Black African communities.[6] One of my favourite writers in this respect is Audre Lorde, a Black feminist lesbian poet, whose work daringly pushes at the boundaries of what is considered 'safe' or acceptable.[7]

In the following dramatic reading, I have attempted to look at this often neglected story from Acts chapter 20 in the light of particular aspects of African Caribbean cultural values and traditions. How might Eutychus have felt or been perceived if he were living within a poor Jamaican family? How would his immediate family, particularly his mother, have viewed his experiences? What about the wider community?

For some of you who have grown up or lived within a Jamaican/Caribbean context, some of what follows may be familiar. For those of you who have been denied such an enriching experience (OK, so I'm biased), then this is a good opportunity to learn more. How might this scenario have been played out in your cultural context or setting?

———◀◦▶———

It Could Have Happened Like This

(A dramatic re-telling of Acts 20:7–11 in an African-Caribbean/Jamaican setting. We see two men and a woman stood in front of a congregation. A Voice off stage begins to read aloud.)

VOICE: From *The Daily Messenger*, Editorial. On the first day of the week, that well-known, popular speaker, Paul of Tarsus, was seen to perform yet another of his miraculous 'healings'. Unconfirmed reports say that a young man named Eutychus, whilst seated at an upstairs window, fell from the window ledge where he was sitting, and was pronounced dead by witnesses. Paul of Tarsus attended to

Eutychus, and soon, quite surprisingly, Eutychus was seen to stand up, quite alive. These events have been the talk of the town since they occurred, yesterday. The authorities are keen to talk to Mr Eutychus, in order that they can hear his side of the story and examine him. Paul of Tarsus, the famous evangelist, has so far refused to talk to the press.

WOMAN: I am Eutychus' mother ... It was my boy who fell from the upstairs window. Do you know how many times I tell that hard-ears bwoy, not fi sit 'pon de window sill? Is wha' dem mek chairs fa? ... (*Turns to Eutychus*) ... It yu mi a' talk to.

EUTYCHUS: My name is Eutychus ... That woman speaking is my mother. I was sitting on the window sill, listening to Paul. He is a good speaker. Not like some of these dry preachers you hear some weeks. Nah man, he was well interesting.

PAUL: I'm Paul, from Tarsus. I was speaking on the night that young Eutychus fell from the window. It came as a shock to me, for something like that to happen, at one of my events.

WOMAN: I've told him time and time again. Don't fall asleep in public and bring a whole heap a' shame 'pon yuself ... So what does the hard-ears pickney go and do? Fall asleep and shame de whole family. Now you have de whole town looking for you ... Stupid bwoy.

EUTYCHUS: I don't remember falling asleep. One minute, I was listening to Paul speaking about Jesus of Nazareth. The room was hot and stuffy. The next, I could feel myself drifting off. My mind began to wander. I imagined I was looking at Jesus. Looking into his eyes, thinking, dreaming. I was in a different world.

WOMAN: Den yu backside lick the floor. See 'im dey? Stiff idiot.

PAUL: One minute, I was speaking, the next, I could see all this commotion taking place at the back of the room. People were running around, shouting, crying. Everyone was very upset. I asked one of my friends what had taken place, and he said that a young boy had fallen from the window. When I went out of the room to where the boy was lying, I was informed that he was dead. I was shocked.

EUTYCHUS: I can't remember much of what happened next. People tell me that I stopped breathing. That I was dead. I don't remember being dead. I don't remember anything.

WOMAN: Yu 'ear dat? 'Im noh remember being dead? Idiot bwoy. Of course not. Yu was dead! Who can remember being dead? I only pray he was wearing clean brief when dis Paul man examine him. Fe my Mumma always tell me, dat yu should always put on clean underwear wen yu leave 'ome, cause yu never know when yu go'n meet accident, and people need to undress you. If yu a' wear dirty brief? ... *(Shakes her head)* ... Pure shame.

EUTYCHUS: I honestly don't remember anything that happened after I hit the ground. I guess, looking back at what happened, I could have gone to meet Jesus of Nazareth. Paul said that Jesus was the Messiah, and all who had faith in him would not die, but would be with him, even after they had died. I think I believe he's the Messiah. I believe in what Paul said.

PAUL: I felt very responsible for what happened that night. I should have tried to control the numbers. But then again, if people want to come to hear the story of Jesus, it is not for me to deny them that opportunity. When I saw young Eutychus, I knew I had to do something, but what? The boy was dead. I couldn't do anything by myself. So I prayed – prayed that God's will would be revealed, and his power be witnessed by everyone who had come to the meeting.

WOMAN: I just didn't know, dat's de frightenin' t'ing about it. My bwoy could a' died, an' I would 'ave known nutting. They would have dragged his body home, told me what happened, and then left him for me to bury. Do you know how hard dat is? For a mother to have to bury her own child? I went tru 15 hours of labour fe dat bwoy. I don't know if I could have done it. Sometimes, life can look very cheap.

EUTYCHUS: I guess I'm lucky. I shouldn't really be here speaking to you today. I should be dead. Exactly where I'd be, I don't know. Hopefully, with Jesus, but who knows?

PAUL: After I had prayed, I leant down by the boy, and looked at him. He looked so peaceful. Sometimes, the only peace some of us find is in death. But I felt Eutychus' time had not come yet. God didn't want him to go. I put my arms around the boy and held him tight. I held him for what seemed like an eternity. I prayed as I held him. I could see all the people standing around, watching me intently; waiting to see what would happen. I could feel the pressure of all their expectations upon me. So I prayed.

WOMAN: If poor Eutychus would a' died, I would ha' fi deal wid all his puppa's family. An' yu see dem? Believe me, yu never see such a bad-living, craven, gravillicous an' tiefing set a' people in yu whole life. Mi only glad, mi nuh ha fi deal wi dem.

EUTYCHUS: I don't know how long I was dead. Some say a few minutes, some say longer. It's weird to be told that you've been raised from the dead. They said it once happened to some guy called Lazarus, but that was years ago. Why me? Why was I so fortunate? What if Paul wasn't there? Makes you think. I could have died, just like that. Still, it's something to tell my friends. I bet many of them can't say they've ever been raised from the dead!

WOMAN: Do you know how many of the neighbours have come 'round to see me, since Eutychus came home? Bwoy, people nosey, hi? Dat woman from next door, she came 'round eight times in one day, asking fi borrow all kin' foolishness. Brushes, boards, feathers, sandals, de kitchen sink. She must t'ink me is fool. I know what's going on. She wants dat hugly, bad-shape daughter of hers fi go out with my Eutychus. Over my dead body. Eutychus is too good for her. After all, he's a celebrity now. He's come back from the dead.

PAUL: When I finished praying, I opened my eyes and looked at Eutychus. His eyes began to open. The life began to trickle back into his face. The people around us began to cheer. Some of them began to pat me on the back. Others congratulated me. Some asked if I had a business card, or if I kept a regular surgery? I tried to tell them, it wasn't me who brought Eutychus back to life. It was by the power of the Living God. I was just the vessel. The messenger. Nothing more.

EUTYCHUS: Things will never be the same. Everything has changed. I'm a celebrity now. A newspaper wants to write a story about me, and how it felt being dead. The local girls won't leave me alone. They all think I'm special, and want to go out with me. My Mum invites over all the relatives and her friends. She charges them money to have their picture taken with me. I don't feel special. Not in that way. But I feel that God is with me. Like wherever I go, God is close at hand. Things will never be the same.

WOMAN: T'ings change fi real. You want to see how people big up this family all of sudden. Mrs Hannah, de bosé one who runs the Women's Guild Fellowship, invited me for tea last week. She thinks me and she is on the same social level now … Things certainly looking up. Eutychus is alright. Still too stupid for my liking, but you know how children stay dese days. De bwoy got religion now. Follows this Paul everywhere. He says his prayers every night. Don't bother me. Personally, if it keep de yout' outta trouble, den dat's alright by me. I'm going to invite Mrs Hannah over to my place next week, to show her my new three-piece suite. Things will never be the same.

PAUL: We had fellowship at the house, after Eutychus had recovered. We ate bread, gave thanks and praised the Lord for the rest of the evening. I still see Eutychus regularly. He attends many of our meetings. He is a very sensitive and intelligent young man. He says that he believes in the risen Christ. I wish him all the best for the future. It won't be easy. Following Christ never is. My ministry continues. I will continue to serve the God of my ancestors, preaching the word, and spreading the good news of Christ's life and death. I seem to be very popular at the moment. I know this popularity won't last, but that isn't important to me. The work must go on. Things change, and always will change. The world will never be the same again.

ALL THREE: The end.

————◄○►————

Post-sketch reflections

Within contemporary life in the West, it is often believed that the sense of cohesion and continuity between peoples, particularly those who share similar backgrounds, has largely broken down. The assumptions one often made about communities and even whole societies sharing narratives that somehow defined and linked people together (often described as 'meta-narratives') have now largely disappeared. The sense of difference and fragmentation that pervades many communities and societies makes the task of chronicling or commenting upon cultural or societal issues very difficult. And yet within African Caribbean cultural life, one is perhaps still able to make those kinds of generalised assumptions. For example, Black people are still more likely to go to church than their White counterparts. And those who attend church are more than likely to share similar cultural and theological backgrounds and perspectives.[8]

African Caribbean people living in Britain are still, perhaps, influenced to a great extent by two dominant themes. These themes have contributed to the continuing sense of homogeneity or sameness that still appears to exist within these communities when compared to other ethnic or cultural groups in the UK. I think these two themes are the ones of 'racism' and 'shame'.

Clearly, given the 'snapshot' framework of this book, it is not possible to offer a detailed analysis of these two themes and the ways in which they continue to exert a powerful influence upon African Caribbean people in Britain. It is worth sharing with you, however, the insights from a small piloting group who have used this sketch.

What emerged from the group was the sense that issues of racism and shame have contributed to Black people utilising a powerful 'internal regulatory' system that polices and defines notions of acceptability, and provides the framework in which communal values and social mores are determined. This internal regulatory system within African Caribbean communities has contributed to an often rigid set of ethics that have governed the lives of these people – myself included.

This group was very conscious of such strictures when analysing the behaviour of the mother in the dramatic reading. All the members knew someone with those kinds of attitudes and forms of behaviour. So how have racism and shame contributed to this reading of the mother when analysing this piece of drama?

In terms of racism, the externalised pressure of being labelled, ridiculed, constricted, oppressed and persecuted has led to many Black people finding it difficult to express healthy disagreement with and criticism of internal forms of behaviour within many of their communities. I have witnessed many Black people, for example, defending Black celebrities whose behaviour would appear to be indefensible. This pilot group found it very difficult to level any criticism at the mother in the drama.[9]

In an effort to provide a solidifying, unified presence in order to counter the worst excesses of racism, many Black communities have been most reluctant to level any blame at those figures or groups whose behaviour is problematic. Commentators who have dared to break free from this seeming strait-jacket of conformity have incurred the wrath of their peers.[10]

The issue of shame emerges as a knock-on effect from the existence of racism. The need to counter racism has led to many Black communities becoming neo-conservative enclaves where the dictates of 'doing the right thing' or being seen to do it take precedence over other concerns. One only has to witness the rigid conformity demanded by many Black-majority churches to see the truth of this phenomenon. For example, personal ethics (particularly involving sexual ethics) are deemed more important than fighting for social justice.[11]

My post-sketch reflections have almost ignored Eutychus and Paul. In many respects, it is the angry caustic figure of the mother who dominates this script. To what extent have my reflections simply replicated the media fascination with particular sections of Black communities – perceiving them as 'exotic', 'problematic' deviants, often at the expense of the majority of law-abiding, decent people? What do you think?

Follow-up questions

Read Acts 20:7–11.

- What is your opinion of Eutychus? Can you identify with his situation and the feelings and thoughts he expresses? If so, why (and if not, then why not)?
- Do you have any sympathy for or kind thoughts about the mother? Why do you think she behaved the way she did?
- If you were Paul and you had to undertake a pastoral visit to Eutychus, and you met his mother, what would you say to her?
- Have you ever found yourself the centre of attention or been perceived as being different, special or unusual for any reason? How did it feel?
- Of the three characters in the sketch, with whom do you most identify, and why?
- Are communities defined by the 'least pleasant' elements amongst their ranks? If yes, then why? If no, then again, why?
- Are there any similarities between this African Caribbean context and your social and cultural situation (assuming it is different to the

sketch)? To what extent are some of the issues at play in this sketch generic of all communities?

- In the light of your own Christian discipleship, what advice would you give Eutychus as he is about to commence with his own faith journey?

PASTORAL CARE AND MINISTRY

In this section I want to investigate the way in which the Christian faith is expressed in terms of pastoral care and sharing, the language of believing and how we relate to and live out the Christian ideals in community.

In this section, as in the later part of the book, when I look at 'Ethics and Action', I am interested in how this intangible and yet intensely real entity called Christianity is lived out and expressed. The Christian faith is not simply a collection of concepts, theories, propositions and doctrines.[1] Obviously, all these elements are very much a part of Christianity, but the Christian faith cannot be reduced to simply being about the ideas or the 'rules' of the faith. Rather, the Christian faith at its most dynamic and penetrating, at its best, is about a lived relationship with Jesus who is the Christ – God Incarnate – God with us![2]

One of the most influential people in the development of my work was the great Grant Shockley. Shockley was for many years the leading Black Christian religious educator in the US. It was the committed work of Shockley that inspired me to want to become a Black religious educator.[3] One of Shockley's most damning assertions was that the Christian Church in North America was wonderful in expressing the rhetoric of faith – that is, talking about the love of Jesus Christ – but was woeful in living out the practical examples of that encounter with him.[4] In the language of popular culture, they 'could talk the talk, but could not walk the walk'.[5]

The importance of the lived expression of the Christian faith cannot be over-estimated. Scholars such as Leslie Francis, Philip Richter[6] and Jeff Astley[7] have identified the extent to which the differences between what people profess and how that profession of faith is lived out can lead to critical levels of emotional and psychological discord. Basically, when the language of faith, the nature of community ('being church') or the examples of pastoral care and mutual support fail to be real or no longer work, then the Christian faith loses a significant amount of its legitimacy. If the things we can see and touch do not work, then to what extent will God's presence be real – especially when the latter cannot often be seen or touched in a direct, literal way?

The sketches and dialogues in this section are an attempt to deal with some of the issues that exist in the daily challenge of living out the Christian faith with and amongst others.

Christian Jargon

Opening reflections

I guess many of us can think of those moments in our lives when a particular event or encounter made a real impression upon us. An impression that later forced us to re-evaluate and reassess what we think or feel about the world. Such a moment happened to me a number of years ago when, as a student at Birmingham University, I took part in an Easter mission in Tipton. It was 1987, and I, along with a group of my peers from the University Meth.Soc., were part of a Street Theatre mission group, sharing the Gospel with the local people of Tipton in the town centre.

It was a hugely influential time in my Christian journey. The Street Theatre mission was great fun. My love for drama and performance was developed during this period of my life. The event that had the profound effect upon me came during an ecumenical evening meeting when I overheard a conversation between a young man who was a member of a local para-church fellowship and a visitor who was not a Christian. The former was trying to explain his understanding of the Christian faith to the visitor. The visitor was interested in learning more about Christianity. He wanted to know why he should believe in Christ.

Every time the visitor posed a question to this Christian man, the latter answered by quoting some stock phrase about Jesus in particular or the faith in general. When the visitor, who did not possess even the most basic idea about the Christian faith, not surprisingly, looked non-plussed and asked another question, seeking clarification, the Christian man replied by using another stock phrase to answer the first one. When the next question duly arrived, the response was yet another cliché. The Christian man did not seem to possess any facility for talking about his faith in a real, non-jargonistic way. One piece of jargon followed the next. This, of course, did not help the visitor in the slightest.

What shocked me as I watched this incident from a slight distance was the fact that I would not have necessarily done any better than this Christian man. If someone had asked me to explain what the Christian faith meant to me at that time, I would have used a series of clichés and jargon-words.

Growing up as I did in a conservative Evangelical church, with a strong emphasis on orthodoxy and traditional Christian belief, I was not nurtured within a context where one asked too many questions or tried to critically interrogate one's faith.

The work of many Pastoral and Practical theologians, particularly in the arena of 'Faith Development Theory',[1] has attempted to enable individuals to reflect upon matters of faith, and to be able to exhibit greater awareness of how that faith works and might be expressed.[2]

Paulo Freire and others have addressed the problem that many poor and oppressed people face in terms of trying to find an authentic language to name their experiences. This is a language that has not been imposed upon them by people who exert power and represent the authority or the establishment.[3]

Christian Jargon was written in order to address some of the issues that had first arisen all those years ago at that meeting in Tipton. It poses the important question that confronts us all. Namely, how do we explain our faith? What words or phrases do we use?

———◦———

Christian Jargon

(We see a solitary figure sitting alone on a chair, centre stage. After a short interval, he/she is joined by another person.)

NO. 2: *(Standing)* Hi ya … How goes it?
NO. 1: *(Looking around shiftily)* Oh … Fine … *(Looking around even more)* Fine.
NO. 2: Anything wrong?
NO. 1: *(Still looking around)* No … I'm … *(Slight pause)* … Fine.
NO. 2: You're sure? It's just that you look a little agitated.

NO. 1: *(Angry)* Look, I said I'm OK ... Is that alright with you?

NO. 2: *(Slight pause)* Not to mention a little tetchy ... You sure you're alright?

NO. 1: *(Rising to his/her feet and glaring at No. 2)* Don't tempt me ...

NO. 2: Alright, alright. No need to get your knickers in a twist ... *(Slight pause)* ... But you are perfectly sure you're alright?

NO. 1: *(About to explode)* Look ...

NO. 2: Hey, calm down, I was only joking ... *(No. 1 returns to his/her seat)* Mind if I join you?

(No. 1 does not answer. No. 2 goes and gets him/herself a seat and sits down.)

NO. 2: *(Pause)* So what's the matter, then?

NO. 1: What is wrong with you? Can't you mind your own business?

NO. 2: No ... So are you going to tell me, then?

NO. 1: You wouldn't be interested.

NO. 2: I wouldn't be asking if I wasn't ... So what's the tale?

NO. 1: No, you wouldn't be ...

NO. 2: Just tell me.

NO. 1: *(Getting to his/her feet and slowly pacing around)* Well ... It's a spiritual problem.

NO. 2: Oh! ... And what is a spiritual problem, then?

NO. 1: It's to do with my faith.

NO. 2: And what is this faith, then?

NO. 1: *(Stops and sits down)* I'm a Christian, you see.

NO. 2: *(Incredulous)* Get out of here ... You, a Christian? Since when?

NO. 1: *(Thinking)* Since I was ... errrm ... 15, I think.

NO. 2: You're having me on. You, a Christian? I've known you since you were three pounds short of being a skeleton, and I never knew. So what is this Christian stuff, then?

NO. 1: Oh, you wouldn't want to know.

NO. 2: Change the record, will you? I'm asking, aren't I?

NO. 1: It's difficult to explain.

NO. 2: Do I look like I'm in a hurry to go anywhere? I'm busy doing nothing ... So open your mouth and just let the words come flowing out.

NO. 1: Well ...

NO. 2: Yes ...?

NO. 1: Well ...

NO. 2: Yes!

NO. 1: Well …

NO. 2: *(Beginning to get excited)* Yes, yes …

NO. 1: Well …

NO. 2: Yes, yes, yes … *(Looking at the audience/congregation)* … This had better be good! … *(Back to No. 1)* … Go on. I'm listening.

NO. 1: Well … Are you sure you want to know?

NO. 2: *(Leaping to his/her feet in exasperation)* Give me strength! Of course I want to know.

NO. 1: Well … I'm a Christian.

NO. 2: *(Patronisingly)* Yes … I think we've established that.

NO. 1: And I believe that the Messiah died for me.

NO. 2: *(Confused)* Wait, wait, wait … Who's this Messiah bloke, then?

NO. 1: The Lord. The King of Kings and the Lord of Lords. The Alpha and Omega. The Light of the World. The Good Shepherd. The Vine. The Living Water.

NO. 2: The who?

NO. 1: What?

NO. 2: What's this Living Water thingy?

NO. 1: The Water of Life. One sip and you'll never be thirsty again.

NO. 2: You mean poison. One sip of that and you'll never be thirsty again … So you believe that poison died for you? Pretty strange idea, don't you think?

NO. 1: What do you mean, poison died for me?

NO. 2: You just said the Messiah died for you. Then you gave me this long list of gobbledygook and you mentioned some Living Water, which I think is poison.

NO. 1: That's not poison, silly. I was talking about the Messiah.

NO. 2: *(Frustrated)* And who is this Messiah, then?

NO. 1: The King of Kings and Lord of Lords. The Alpha and Omeg–

NO. 2: *(Leaping to his/her feet)* Not that again! … Look, in words of one syllable or less, kindly tell me who this Messiah chappie is who died for you … Or something like that.

NO. 1: *(Looking at No. 2 suspiciously)* Well …

NO. 2: And I want none of that incomprehensible babble, either.

NO. 1: *(Slowly)* The Messiah … was … *(very quickly)* the Son of God.

NO. 2: The Son of God? Really? I see … Who are the King of Kings and the Lord of Lords, then? His brothers?

NO. 1: No, silly. They're the same person.

NO. 2: All the same person? What's with all the names? Get confused about his identity, did he?

NO. 1: Don't you dare be sacrilegious about my Saviour!

NO. 2: Who's this Saviour, then?

NO. 1: That's the same person again.

NO. 2: How many names does this person go by? Are there any other names I should know about?

NO. 1: *(Slightly reticent)* Well ... You could call him Jesus.

NO. 2: *(Begins to pace around)* So let me get this right ... You believe that this Messiah died for you ... who, as it happens, also goes by the name of King of Kings, Lord of Lords ... Alph– *(Struggling with the next word)* ... Alph–

NO. 1: Alpha and Omega.

NO. 2: *(Looking at No. 1 momentarily)* Alpha and Omega, Saviour, and now Jesus ... Right! So we've established that much. This man of many names died for you ... Now for my second question. Why?

NO. 1: To reconcile all people to God.

NO. 2: To what?

NO. 1: Man – or should I say people – have slipped from the paths of righteousness and have delved into a life of sin.

NO. 2: Whow ... Steady on there, Trigger ... Rewind, rewind. What's this righteousness and sin, then? Are they related to this Messiah bloke? The Lord of Lords and King of ...

NO. 1: No, silly ... They have nothing to do with the Messiah ... Well, righteousness does, but the Messiah has no truck with sin. He cannot abide sin. That's why he died for our sins.

NO. 2: And how did he do that?

NO. 1: By ransoming his soul that we may be free.

NO. 2: Free from what?

NO. 1: From a life of sin.

NO. 2: And what's this sin, then?

NO. 1: Hmmmmm ... I'm not rightly sure, but it gets a big mention in the New Testament.

NO. 2: *(Very confused)* Right ... So this Me– ... What's his name again?

NO. 1: Messiah.

NO. 2: Yeah, him. Also known as the King of Kings and Lord of

Lords. Alias the Alpha and Omega, the Saviour and Jesus. He died for your sins. To take you away from a life of sin, because you had slipped from the paths of righteousness. How am I doing so far?

NO. 1: Fine.

NO. 2: So ... What happens now?

NO. 1: Now that I have been washed in the blood of the Lamb ...

NO. 2: *(Shocked)* The what?

NO. 1: *(Undeterred)* The blood of the Lamb. I have been saved. My soul is now reconciled with God and my name will be etched in the gilded pages of the Lamb's book of life. And when I die, my soul will ascend to heaven, where I will dine in the house of the Lord for ever and ever, and eat and drink of the milk and the wine.

NO. 2: *(Long pause)* That's nice ... I didn't understand a word of it, but it sounds really lovely. Just one thing I don't understand ... Well, lots of things actually, but I'll start with this one ... What has the Lamb's blood got to do with anything? And what happens if you're a vegetarian?

NO. 1: It's all very simple. Look, I'll take you through it all again. In the beginning was the Word, and the Word was God. The Word was ...

NO. 2: What's this Word, then? Not a dirty word, is it?

NO. 1: No ... The Word was Jesus, who existed with God and the Holy Ghost.

NO. 2: *(Incredulous)* The Holy Ghost! Well, if you are going to talk about ghosts, then this seems like the ideal time for me to be going. Me and ghost stories don't go together.

(No. 2 gets to his/her feet and is ready to leave.)

NO. 1: Hey, don't go. Don't you want to hear how you can renounce your old life and find new hope in the Incarnate Christ?

NO. 2: *(Walking away)* No thanks. It sounds far too complicated for me. I passed my 'O' Level English, but this is still double Dutch.

NO. 1: *(Rising to his/her feet to follow No. 2)* It's really very simple. It's only taken me 20 years of church attendance to understand it. There's really nothing to it ... And besides, don't you want to hear about my spiritual problems?

(No. 2 has now left the stage ... He/she is out of sight.)

NO. 2: Write it down in an essay and I'll read it when I need to catch up on some sleep.

NO. 1: *(Walking off stage)* Oh well … Please yourself.

THE END

———◄○►———

Post-sketch reflections

I have a confession to make – this is my favourite script in this book. My reasons for liking it are not hard to fathom. In many respects, it speaks to the very heart of our religious consciousness. Who is God for us? Given the claims Christian theology makes for the personal relationship the individual can attain with God in Christ, in the power of the Holy Spirit, a more pointed question is, 'Who is Jesus for us?'[4]

Quite naturally, this script has elicited a great deal of comment from the various groups with whom it has been used. Many issues have arisen around the question of religious language. Religious scholars as diverse as William James,[5] through to more recent contributions by my colleague at Queens, Adam Hood,[6] and from a Diasporan African context, in the form of Anthony Pinn,[7] have all looked at the phenomenon of religious experience and language.

This sketch was written prior to my training as an educator and a theologian, but it nevertheless echoed the struggles I was going through at that time in my own faith formation. To what extent did the lexicon of classical Christianity work for me? Were the words and the accompanying concepts fine, but simply lacking a new set of terms or language in which to house them, or was there a fundamental problem with the very concepts and formulas themselves?

When I began to undertake participatory research with predominantly marginalised lay people in the West Midlands area and in London, I returned to this sketch as a means of re-investigating this ongoing struggle.

The groups who have used this sketch have fallen neatly into two broad categories. In the first category are those for whom the issue is one primarily concerned with presentation. It is not the central concepts around Jesus and his work (Soteriology) or his person (Christology) that are in question, but the ways in which these categories or concepts have been presented. Many of these individuals tend to live within what might be termed a broadly Evangelical camp.[8] The responses of these individuals accord with the work of such scholars as Andrew Walker[9] or the whole 'Alpha' phenomenon. Essentially, one is not in the business of deconstructing the traditional or classical heart of Christianity; rather, these authors are attempting to find a more conducive receptacle in which the faith can be housed and propagated.

For others, the failure of the words used by character No. 1 in the script is simply the tip of a deconstructionist iceberg. The presentation is not itself the problem (although, quite naturally, it does not help), but rather, the failure of the words is simply a reflection of a wider malaise. Namely, that people have moved away, quite significantly in some cases, from the credal building blocks of classical Christianity. Many who have responded in this way to the sketch are largely from a broadly Liberal perspective. The struggles with both the language and the underlying concepts that underpin these terms accord with some of the pertinent issues that have been raised by a number of scholars, particularly those who are within a critical Liberationist perspective.[10]

These seemingly opposing issues have been reflected by those who have engaged with this sketch. What has emerged most convincingly from my encounters with those who have used the script has been the positive identification many have made with Jesus. The one who is the 'Word' remains a hugely captivating figure, whether approached as an 'above' symbol, as the Christ of faith (i.e. his universal work of salvation is paramount), or as a 'below' figure, as the Jesus of history. The figure who is at the heart of Christianity continues to draw people to himself and to inspire and demand not only worship but also critical solidarity with those with whom he was most concerned.

Follow-up questions

Read Matthew 16:13–20. Look also at the Apostles' Creed (you can find a version of it in most church worship/liturgy books). Then consider the following questions:

• Jesus asks his followers 'Who do you say I am?' How would you answer that question?

- If you had to describe the basis of your faith in about 100 words, what would you write or say?
- Character No. 1 in the sketch uses a variety of terms to describe Jesus. Which of these terms (if any) work for you? Why do they work or make sense? Which do not, and if not, then why not?
- Looking at the Apostles' Creed, if you had to choose three phrases from it that summed up the Christian faith for you, what would they be and why?
- If you had to select only one phrase from those three, which would it be and why?
- How has your faith changed since you first became a Christian?
- How has it changed in the last year?
- In the last six months?

A Problem Shared

Opening reflections

Some of the strangest ironies I have seen and faced in my active involvement in the Church have been the occasions when the Church has attempted to act in solidarity with and identity with the poor and marginalised in society. To be clear at this point, I am not suggesting that the Church is not sincere in its desire to be alongside those who are often disaffected and disillusioned, due to a host of economic and social factors that leave them on the margins of society. Initiatives such as the Church Urban Fund (Church of England) and Mission Alongside the Poor (Methodist) have played a significant role not only in attempting to alleviate the causes of poverty, but also in increasing the awareness of such issues amongst the mainly middle-class clientele who inhabit most of our churches.

The irony that often overwhelms me when the Church engages in this type of conversation is due in no small measure to the personnel who are present when such discussions are taking place. On such occasions, when we are talking about poverty and marginalisation, there is usually no one who falls into that category in the room when the discussion is taking place. In effect, we talk about particular groups of people, or talk for them, but we rarely talk with them.

Scholars such as Kenneth Leech[1] and John Vincent[2] have sought to locate the radical teachings of Jesus as being at the heart of the Gospel, and in accordance with his actions, the poor have been accorded a place of privilege. The work of liberation theologians such as Gustavo Gutteriez[3] and the Boff brothers[4] has been a radical challenge to the whole Christian Church. They have helped us all to see the Gospel as best understood in terms of being a political and spiritual movement that will enable the poor and the oppressed to live real lives as full human subjects in this world. In this respect, their work, and that of many others, has reminded the Church that dialogue and solidarity with those who are poor is not an added optional extra, but is at the heart of what most concerned Jesus' ministry.

When the following dialogue was first written I was unemployed. I remember how isolated I felt, as many of my comfortable, middle-class friends (inside and outside the Church) did not know how to relate to me. I think they were more embarrassed for me than I was of myself. In the intervening time, since this piece was first written, Emmanuel Lartey's work on inter-cultural approaches to pastoral care has done much to enable us to see how Christian care and concerns can be made effective across diverse backgrounds and settings.[5]

A key concept in any approach to crossing boundaries in order to establish links with those on the margins is a commitment to community. And community begins with conversation – a commitment to naming and affirming our differences.[6]

One of the challenges that have confronted me upon re-reading this dialogue is related to my own 'comfort zones'. Where are my lines of exclusion drawn? With whom am I not comfortable? Do I associate with people who are mostly like me, and who make me feel good? Consider some of these questions as you read and perform the following dialogue.

————◄◦►————

A Problem Shared

(A dramatic reading for two people.)

NO. 1: I am very fortunate. God has blessed me abundantly.

NO. 2: I am very unfortunate. God seems to have cursed my life. I have the type of fortune which makes Job look like a lucky person.

NO. 1: Being a person blessed by God, I see the world through glasses with the most rose-tinted lenses you ever saw.

NO. 2: The kind of life I have, I don't even have glass in my spectacles.

NO. 1: I think life is wonderful … I'm so very happy.

NO. 2: They said to me, 'Smile, things can't get any worse.' So I did smile … And things did get worse.

NO. 1: I can see my life extending out into the distance and the future looks wonderful.

NO. 2: Life is a swine and then you die. What more is there to say?

NO. 1: They say that the meek shall inherit the earth.

NO. 2: Of course they will! Six feet of it.

NO. 1: I have a wonderful job, which is satisfying, enjoyable and very well paid.

NO. 2: I have no job, I'm unemployed.

NO. 1: Because I have a wonderful job, people listen to me. They take notice of what I say, consider my opinion and respect my views.

NO. 2: People either ignore me, or they patronise me. I'm either smothered with bleeding hearts and do-gooding sentiments, or they run away from me, fearing my presence will embarrass them. Wonderful, isn't it?

NO. 1: I do sometimes feel slightly guilty at the way my life has worked out. Why am I so fortunate? How come so many good things seem to happen to me?

NO. 2: I sometimes wonder what terrible thing I did to God, for all this bad luck to hit me. I mean, I'm not that bad a person, am I? I don't think so.

NO. 1: I would like to think that I am a patient and understanding person.

NO. 2: I would like to meet a patient and understanding person. But I've got the plague and no one wants to talk to me.

NO. 1: I find that my guilt is no good in itself. Being guilty never changed anything. I would like to be of help to those less fortunate than myself.

NO. 2: I've yet to meet anyone less fortunate than myself. If I did, I wouldn't know what to say to them. I'd probably depress them. I depress me ... all the time.

NO. 1: I find the difficulty in trying to help people, is knowing where to start. You can't just walk into someone's life, invade their space and get them to tell you all their troubles ... *(Slight pause)* ... Not unless you want an earful of abuse.

NO. 2: I wouldn't know where to start ... I suppose my being unemployed gives me time enough to sit down and write out all my troubles. Problem is, once I get started, I wouldn't know when to stop. I could be writing for months. It would make a very long and boring book.

NO. 1: I suppose I could slip quietly beside the person concerned, push a cup of tea into their hand, smile, and then get them to tell me their entire life story.

NO. 2: If there is one thing I hate, it's those do-gooders who sneak up to you after church services, with a cup of tea in one hand and a big cheesy grin in the other. They hand you the tea and then ask you to tell them your life story. It's worse than being on *This is Your Life.*

NO. 1: The problem is … if the other person doesn't open up, you can't really understand or share their problem. I don't know what to do. I'd hate to say the wrong thing.

NO. 2: I'd feel silly telling my problems to someone else. No one wants to be that depressed, do they? And if I did start talking, I'm sure they would be judging me. Looking at me. Wondering why I'm not working. Trying to guess how I manage. Do you know that there are still individuals who think people like me are scroungers? I think the modern term is 'lounge lizard'. I have been known to lounge around, but I wouldn't describe myself as a lizard. Well, not during daylight hours, anyway.

NO. 1: As a Christian, I suppose it is my duty to be caring and under-standing. I do try. But … it's … it's … I … I always feel uncomfort-able around people who are not having a good time of it. It's as if I'm personally responsible. And in a way, I suppose I am. We are meant to be responsible for each other, aren't we?

NO. 2: I'm not quite sure if I want to be responsible to other people. It's as if they own a piece of you. But I suppose we are meant to be one family. And families should talk and air their problems. Looks like I don't have a choice.

NO. 1: I don't care what they say … I'm going to ask them if there is any-thing I can do to help. I might get my head bitten off, but I don't care. I've got to ask.

NO. 2: Should I tell someone about my being unemployed, or should I wait for them to approach me with the cup of tea and the cheesy grin? Decisions, decisions.

NO. 1: I'm going to do it. I'll get the tea and polish my teeth. I hope my breath doesn't smell.

NO. 2: Here they come … I can see the tea and the big grin. Lord, be with me.

NO..1: I've got the tea and my pearly white teeth are on display. I'm on my way.

(No. 1 begins to approach No. 2.)

NO. 2: He/she's on his/her way.

NO. 1: Here I come.

NO. 2: I can't run away now.

NO. 1: Point of no return.

NO. 2: This is it.

NO. 1: This is it.

NOS. 1 & 2: Hello.

NO. 1: I was wondering if you are alright? Hope I'm not intruding.

NO. 2: No, of course not. Good of you to ask.

NO. 1: Would you like a cup of tea?

NO. 2: Thank you.

THE END

———◄○►———

Post-sketch reflections

One of the consequences of the personalised, subjective spirituality that is inherent within aspects of Pauline theology has been the development of a range of accompanying or 'knock-on' attributes that arise from this tradition. In short, Paul's emphasis upon the reforming and regulatory work of the Spirit has instilled within many Christian believers many of the attributes that in turn lead to social and economic advancement.

The hot-house atmosphere of religious fervour and social change that characterised the holiness movement within the eighteenth- and nineteenth-century Evangelical revivals led to significant developments in the moral, spiritual and social advancement of the urban poor in Britain.[7] Having grown up within the Methodist Church in Britain, I can attest, personally, to the dour, dutiful and earnest climate of holiness that stained the atmosphere of the gathered community of faith that was Eastbrook Hall in Bradford, West Yorkshire. Rupert Davies' popular book, which charts the historical developments of Methodism, highlights the potency of Wesley's teaching on holiness and its efficacy on the religious sensibilities of his initial eighteenth-century followers.[8]

Later generations within Methodism, along with many of her free-church relatives and her 'established' elder sibling, were active participants in the development of social and educational programmes for the betterment of the poor and deprived. In the latter arena of education, Cliff's work on the rise and development of the Sunday School Union charts the important contributions made by Christian faith communities to the creation of educational opportunities for those outside the orbit of seeming privilege, comfort and affluence.[9]

My education about and induction into the Christian faith was imbued with an aspirant, self-improvement ethic that lay at the forefront of my heightened religious awareness. I grew up in a church atmosphere that was a highly competitive arena. It was a place of self-improvement and progress.

I make these reflections because, in using this sketch with a number of groups, it has been interesting to see how many of the participants have stated that they came from working-class backgrounds. Essentially, Christian faith appears to be a useful transformative process, which leads to social and economic advancement.[10] This advancement naturally leads to a form of progress that separates us from the very people with whom we may feel some form of commitment and to whom we have some form of affinity.

When I first wrote this sketch, I was struck by how 'twee' and trite it appeared. I was a little embarrassed by it, but as the writing simply reflected where my thoughts and feelings were leading me, I felt obliged to leave the piece as it was. Having visited South Africa for the first time last year, and having used this sketch there with a number of people, I have been struck by how challenging is the simple act of trying to talk as an equal with someone else who is not like you. It is comparatively easy to ignore those who are poor and not in your social circle. It is equally easy to talk down to others. It is relatively hard to talk with others in such a way as to enhance their dignity and self-esteem.

A number of people who have engaged with this sketch have wondered how an entrenched middle-class institution like the Church can relate to those who are poor, whether they are inside or outside the life of the many Christian communities in the UK. Some people have felt that the very process of engaging in this drama and attempting to climb into the experience of others provided a helpful start to any process of attempting to be in solidarity with others. It has to be acknowledged, however, that many remained sceptical and critical. Some felt that this process (which begins with this sketch) rarely leads to any significant change in terms of how individuals and the institution seriously engage with those who are poor.

Follow-up questions

Read Matthew 25:31–46 and Luke 10:25–37.

- Draw a series of concentric circles. In the innermost circle write down the names of the people to whom you are the closest. In the next circle out, write down the next set of names – the people to whom you are the closest after those in the innermost circle. Continue until all the names of the people with whom you associate are placed in one of the circles – i.e. the smaller the circle, the closer to them you are (or they to you).
- Look at the above circles and names. How many of these people are similar to you in some way? If so, then how? How many are different? Again, how are they different?
- How do you interpret the various names in the above circles in the light of the two Gospel passages?
- In both Gospel passages, Jesus challenges those around him to cross cultural, social or religious barriers in order to act in solidarity with others. What or where are the barriers that prevent you from acting in solidarity with others?
- Think of one practical action you could take in order to be alongside and supportive of another person or group who are different from you. What is it, and how will you commit yourself to this action?
- Have you benefited economically and materially from being a Christian? If so, then how? If not, then why not?
- To what extent does being in the Church provide the basis for your social life and broader lifestyle?

Ministry of the Whole People of God in the World

Opening reflections

This sketch was written for a Methodist circuit service in Birmingham, where the theme was collaborative ministry – the joint working out of Christian discipleship between all people, whether lay or ordained. A number of years prior to this service, the Methodist Church had issued a report entitled *The Ministry of the People of God* (1986), which, amongst a number of issues, addressed the question of collaborative ministry. This report had been preceded by another report entitled *Sharing in God's Mission* (1985).

In writing this sketch, I wanted to address one of the perennial issues in many of our churches – namely, that a relatively small group of people find themselves having to undertake all the work in the church. This group of people usually end up feeling tired, worn out and de-motivated. The effect upon the ordained minister is equally acute, as stress levels and fatigue sap many women and men of their enthusiasm and energy. It must be noted, however, that some clergy do not help themselves, by assuming responsibility for doing everything within the church. Many are much too insecure to allow lay people to assume any serious measure of responsibility or power.

In many respects, this sketch encapsulates the central idea running through this book – namely, that the work of the Kingdom is much too important to be left solely in the hands of those who are ordained or highly educated and recognised lay people. In actual fact, it is when the laity are empowered, educated and enabled to express their true potential and their often submerged and repressed talents that the Church becomes more effective in her witness and ministry to the world. The likes of Jeff Astley[1] and Grant Shockley[2] have made a number of telling comments on the desirability or otherwise, of lay people being educated to take responsibility for their own faith journeys and Christian discipleship.

The following sketch is a challenge to all people of faith to engage with the communities, the people and the surroundings in which we move, breathe and have our being. Too often, Christian faith is seen as a safety buffer against the world and all that it represents. Rather than being an affirming and empowering resource that enables us to tackle the world head on, we instead use the Christian faith as an excuse to withdraw and disengage. Our withdrawal is hugely ironic, given that we often assert that the whole of creation belongs to God, for it was created by God. If the latter point is true, then our withdrawal and disengagement is not only a betrayal of trust, but is also an example of bad stewardship.

As a Black Methodist theologian, I am reminded that Wesley regarded the whole world as his parish and would not countenance any attempt by the early Methodists to separate themselves from the needs of the whole of society.[3]

I hope that *Ministry of the Whole People of God in the World* will challenge us all in our continuing Christian discipleship.

————◄○►————

Ministry of the Whole People of God in the World

(On stage we see five chairs ... Enter the Captain, with a mock dog collar around his neck. He walks forward to address the congregation/audience.)

CAPTAIN: Welcome, ladies and gentlemen, to the good ship *The Christian Church.* Our mission is to boldly go where other ships have not gone before. To seek out the lost, the lonely, the sad, the bereaved and the hurt. We are to be the salt of the world. That candle on the hill. The ... *(Forgets what to say next)* ... The ... You get the picture ... Well, without further ado, we join the crew on the bridge of the good ship *The Christian Church.*

(With this, the Captain turns around and walks towards the empty chairs. Whilst he is doing so, four other characters walk onto the stage. All five take their seats.)

CAPTAIN: Well, team, this is it. The big one. The moment of truth. Out there lies the world. A world simply waiting to be told about the good news. And we, team ... *(Looks around at the other four)* ... we have that news. Our job is to go out there and minister to all those around us.

NO. 1: Why?

CAPTAIN: Why? Did I hear you say why?

NO. 1: Yes, Boss ... Why do we have to go out there ...? Why can't they come inside here and join us? There's enough room for everyone.

NO. 2: We've had new carpets put in and satellite TV.

NO. 3: Don't forget the jacuzzi.

NO. 4: Or the potted plants.

NO. 1: Or the Billy Graham boxed set of memorable sermons.

NO. 2: Not forgetting the Charles Wesley karaoke sing-a-long special.

NOS. 1, 2, 3 & 4: *(In unison)* What more could they want?

CAPTAIN: *(Rising to his feet ... Begins to pace around)* I don't believe I'm hearing this ... Why? Why do we have to go out into the world? Is that what I'm hearing? ... *(The other four all look shame-faced)* ... Why don't they come in here? Did you learn nothing at Sunday School training college? Of course we have to go out into the world. That is our mission. That is why we are here.

NO. 2: *(Slight pause)* But it's so nasty and horrible out there.

NO. 1: The people aren't polite and courteous like in here.

NO. 3: Last time I went outside, this woman laughed at me. She said I looked like a wally.

NO. 4: *(To No. 3)* But you *are* a wally.

NO. 3: I know I am, but I didn't want her telling me.

NO. 2: We get no respect out there. A man cannot live without respect.

CAPTAIN: You have to earn respect.

NO. 2: That's easy for you to say ... You've got that magic piece of white cardboard around your neck. That makes all the difference.

NOS. 1, 3 & 4: Yeah, it does.

CAPTAIN: No it doesn't.

NOS. 1, 2, 3 & 4: Oh yes it does.

CAPTAIN: No it doesn't.

NOS. 1, 2, 3 & 4: Oh yes it–

CAPTAIN: Alright, that's enough of that ... What do you think this is, a pantomime? Look, it shouldn't make any difference. We are all equipped to go out there and do this job. We are all ministers. We all have a ministry to exercise. We've all got access to the Holy Spirit lighter fuel, and you all know where the tool cupboard is, to get hold of your armour-of-God hand-kit. You can all play your part.

NO. 1: Do we have to?

NOS. 1, 2, 3 & 4: Do we have to?

CAPTAIN: *(Rising to his feet again)* Do we have to go through all this again? We all have our parts to play. If this mission is going to be successful, if the good ship *The Christian Church* is going to complete its mission, then each and every one of us will need to do his or her bit. You remember what the Controller said about the body and the many parts?

NOS. 1, 2, 3 & 4: Not that again!

NO. 2: I've heard that story so many times I can recite it in my sleep.

NO. 3: I keep waking up thinking I'm a nose ... full of cold.

CAPTAIN: Look, I can't do this mission by myself. You all have a ministry and the world out there is waiting to see it. So are you going out there or not?

NOS. 1, 2, 3 & 4: *(Looking around at each other)* Suppose so.

CAPTAIN: Good, I'll brief you all.

NO. 4: What do we have to do? I keep forgetting.

NO. 1: Me too.

CAPTAIN: You simply be yourself. Nothing more, nothing less. Wherever you are, you live your life in the best way you know how.

NO. 2: Is that it?

CAPTAIN: Yes, that's it ...

NO. 3: What's the point of that?

CAPTAIN: The best way of telling people about our mission is to attempt to live out the truths you have been told. That is your ministry, to live ordinary lives in the world, being yourself.

NO. 4: I don't know who I am. Can't I be someone else?

NO. 1: And why do we have to go to our everyday environment and be ordinary? I'd rather go to Florida and be special. I'm sure I'd work more effectively if the Controller sent me to Brazil.

NO. 2: Or Jamaica.

NO. 3: Copacobana Beach. Now I could do some serious ministry over there, I can tell you.

NO. 1: If you give me the tickets, I can be over in the sun in two shakes of a lamb's tail. I'll do a brilliant job. Don't worry, I'll send you a postcard.

NOS. 1, 2, 3 & 4: Me too, me too.

CAPTAIN: Hold on a minute ... Who do you think the Controller is, your ready-made travel agent? You have to go into your natural, everyday environment.

NO. 1: But why?

NOS. 2, 3 & 4: Yeah, why?

CAPTAIN: Because people know you there. Your presence will make a difference. Your life will make a difference. No one would know who you were in Copacobana Beach.

NO. 2: We'd have a good time.

CAPTAIN: But life isn't simply about having a good time. It's about being faithful.

NO. 4: Spoilsport!

(There follows a slight interlude ... All is silent.)

CAPTAIN: Are we all ready to go out there and exercise our ministries?

NOS. 1, 2, 3 & 4: *(Reluctantly)* Suppose so.

CAPTAIN: You don't have to look so cheerful about it.

NO. 3: What is there to be cheerful about?

NO. 1: The Controller is throwing us out into that nasty, grimy-looking world, and you expect us to be happy?

CAPTAIN: The Controller never said it would be easy.

NO. 2: Make us more depressed, why don't you?

NO. 4: This is going to be a bundle of laughs, I can see it right now.

(The Captain leaps to his feet and begins to gee up the other four.)

CAPTAIN: Come on, team ... The world awaits ... No time like the present. Into the world we must go.

NO. 1: *(Sarcastically)* With a skip and a jump and a ho ho ho.

(The other four slowly get to their feet.)

CAPTAIN: OK, gang ... In your own time. Operation Ministry of the Whole People of God in the World will commence ... I'll count us down ... Five, four, three, two, one and a half, one and a quarter, one ... zero ... Off you go! I'll follow in a minute.

(Nobody moves.)

CAPTAIN: Come on, team ... Play the game ... Let's go.

(Slowly, the other four begin to walk off stage in different directions,

leaving the Captain alone. After a short interval, we hear the voice of No. 3 calling out.)

NO. 3: *(Out of sight)* Can't I have a dog collar like you? I'd be much better with a dog collar.

CAPTAIN: You'll be better off without one. People respect ordinary human beings. No one respects dog collars – not even me.

NO. 1: *(Also out of sight)* Are you sure I can't go to Copacobana Beach? I really could do some damage out there on that lovely golden sand.

CAPTAIN: No, you'll enjoy yourself much more amongst your friends in your own neighbourhood.

NO. 1: Awww … Spoilsport.

NO. 4: Do I have to be myself? Why can't I be some famous Christian? I hate being me.

CAPTAIN: But other people will respect you for being yourself, rather than trying to impersonate someone else. You'll do fine.

NO. 2: *(Running back to meet the Captain)* I'm scared …

CAPTAIN: *(Beginning to walk away with an arm around No. 2)* So am I … So am I …

(Exit the Captain and No. 2 … Silence …)

THE END

Post-sketch reflections

On the occasions when this sketch has been used, I have been struck by the extent to which lay and ordained people see the world of Christian ministry in similar ways, but for very different reasons. For many lay people, they have been amused by the actions and attitude of the 'Captain' in the sketch. Some have said that 'He [an assumption on their part] seems OK, but we've seen few of them [ministers] who are prepared to challenge and give away power like that.'

When I have spoken with ministers, they have often smiled ruefully (a couple have laughed themselves into near hysteria) at the actions of the Captain in the sketch. Many have perceived the Captain as being much too naïve and simplistic in his actions.

What has been agreed by both sets of people is the need for increased education and training for lay people in order that they can be equipped to take on more responsibility and leadership roles in the Church. Part of the difficulty in that process is the relatively low level of theological thinking and reflection amongst lay people in many of our churches. A number of Christian educators and Practical theologians have been concerned with the need to develop new strategies and methods for raising the theological consciousness of lay people. The work of Black scholars such as Grant Shockley,[4] Lynne Westfield[5] and Anne Wimberly[6] has been supplemented by White scholars such as John Hull,[7] Mary Elizabeth Moore[8] and Jeff Astley.[9]

Within many struggling and marginalised contexts where the development of a type of critical Christianity has emerged, it has been interesting to note that the emphasis in its formation has been very much upon the training and education of clergy. The needs of lay people have been seen as secondary at best and a marginal issue at worst.[10]

The issue of how we enable lay people to feel better equipped to take on responsibility for church leadership also poses a number of critical questions for those involved in the initial and continued training of ordained clergy. One of the most critical issues to arise from their engagement with this sketch has been related to the identity of ministers. How do ministers perceive and understand their roles? To what extent is their role dependent upon 'being in charge' – an exercising of authority that negates the possibility of lay leadership? For some ministers, their role is understood primarily in terms of utility – that is, being very much preoccupied with doing 'useful' things in order to justify one's role.

In more recent times, increasing attention has been directed at addressing critical questions to the theology and related work of ordained ministry. In Luscombe's and Shreeve's book, it has been interesting to see the varied understandings and perceptions of ordained ministry.[11] Commendably, there is a balance between ordained and lay perspectives.[12] It has been interesting to relate some of the reflections of the different groups who have engaged with this sketch with those of the various authors in Luscombe's and Shreeve's book. To what extent does the Church really take seriously the notion of collaboration between lay and ordained in the Church?[13]

Follow-up questions

Read: Romans 12:1–12.

- What are the connections between the sketch and the passage from Romans? What does the passage say about our understanding of collaborative ministry?
- Reflecting upon the passage (in addition to thinking about the sketch), what is your understanding of the individual responsibilities of every Christian believer?
- If your friends or family members had to describe you to a complete stranger, what might they say were your gifts or talents? What makes you unique? (We are all unique.)
- In terms of the above, what would you say was your distinctive ministry?
- How can we enable lay and ordained people to work together more effectively in ministry? What are your thoughts on the relationship between the Captain and the other characters in the sketch?
- In order that your ministry might be more effective, what can you and/or your church do to equip you?

RACIAL JUSTICE /
BLACK THEOLOGY

As a Black Christian educator and theologian, one of my major areas of commitment and involvement has been that of racial justice. Both disciplines of Black Christian education and Black theology contain within them an explicit and implicit concern for those historic, structural forces and attitudes that have affected Black people and other people of colour. Scholars such as Robert Beckford[1] and Samuel Yeboah[2] have highlighted the dynamic and changeable nature of racism. The phenomenon of racism can be likened to that of a verb rather than a noun – it is a 'doing entity' that is active rather than a passive object.

The drafting of legislation by many Western governments in order to counter and even eradicate racism has only led to incremental or marginal changes, because whilst laws are often rigid and inflexible, racism has proved itself to be supremely flexible. Two extreme examples of this phenomenon can be seen in the United States and in South Africa. In the former, it is 40 years since Civil Rights legislation outlawed crude institutional racism,[3] yet the economic and social conditions that affect the majority of African Americans remain largely unchanged.

Similarly, within South Africa, the new universal democratic dispensation now sanctioned in a visionary all-inclusive constitution has been unable to deal with the flexibility of racism as practised by many White South Africans. Often, the drafting of law, which can be likened to the fixed festival of Christmas, has been met with the elusive racism of White supremacy that can be compared to the movable feast of Easter.

The work of racial justice specialists[4] continues to remind our various churches that tackling and opposing racism is not an optional extra in the work for the Kingdom of God.[5] As I hope to demonstrate in the various exercises and sketches, racial justice lies at the heart of the Gospel of Christ.

Various individuals and organisations wanting to find accessible and interactive ways of helping non-specialists to get to grips with some of the major concerns in this area of Christian witness and challenge, commissioned much of the following material. I have updated this material, adding new references and ideas in order to respond to some of the changes that have emerged since this work was first written.

In many respects, this section of the book is probably the most challenging, as it highlights an area of concern that many of us would prefer to ignore or overlook. If I had a pound for every time I have heard the now immortal phrase, 'We don't have a problem here, as we don't have any Black members', I could use that money to take an expensive holiday. In answer to that often-used phrase, I will state, quite categorically, that Black people are not a problem, but an opportunity. As I stated in my previous book,[6] Black people are not and have never been the 'problem'. Rather, racism and the accompanying attitudes of superiority and exploitation that have undermined and bedevilled us all, continue to be the great 'problems' for everyone. After all, it was the great W. E. B. Dubois who stated that the problem of the twentieth century was the problem of the colour line.[7] We have yet to get to grips with Dubois' analysis of racism from the last century!

The material in this section of the book is an attempt to get us beyond the helpful but ultimately inflexible response of legislation and top-down sanction, to a more flexible theological approach that is bound up in the generosity and fluid dimension that is Easter – a movable feast that responds to the cycle of the moon and nature.

Stakeholding

Opening reflections

> All human beings are born free and equal in dignity and rights.
> They are endowed with reason and conscience and should act
> towards one another in a spirit of brotherhood. Everyone is en-
> titled to all the rights and freedoms set forth in this Declaration,
> without distinction of any kind, such as 'race', colour, sex,
> language, religion, political or other opinion, national or social
> origin, birth or other status.[1]

So begins the 1948 Universal Declaration of Human Rights. The opening phrase of that statement is a very powerful and compelling one. Few
would argue with the rhetoric. In more recent times, Tony Blair has
spoken of a notion he has termed 'stakeholding'. This idea is one in
which people of differing backgrounds, ethnicities, creeds, class,
education and so forth are given the tools (primarily through education
and training) and are empowered in order that they can become full
stakeholders in this society. This ideal is one that attempts to enable all
people to stake their claim within Britain, in terms of participation in
the wealth, advantages, opportunities and progress of this country.
Access to the opportunities and possibilities of living in Britain carries
with it responsibilities, in addition to the aforementioned rights. This
initiative is no less compelling than the Universal Declaration I quoted
previously.

I have chosen the theme of stakeholding in order to highlight a
number of issues and factors that hinder and prevent this ideal of all
people being able to stake their claim on this country. For whilst there
has been an informal and often unspoken belief in the notion of Britain
being a nation of 'fair play' and good old-fashioned decency, it has been
the case that racism has prevented many people from being full

stakeholders in this country. In post-colonial Britain, particularly in the era when the mass migratory movement of Black and Asian people came to Britain, countless numbers of these people found their opportunities to stake a claim on this country being denied them. Stakeholding has been a nice ideal, but one that was more of a pipe-dream than actual reality.

If one looks at contemporary Britain, one will see a variety of examples of how the concept of stakeholding has been denied to many people. If one thinks of Stephen Lawrence, we have the most graphic and extreme example of a person being denied the opportunity to be a stake-holder. To put it bluntly, you cannot be a stakeholder if you are denied your life. Dead people cannot make any claim or demand any rights!

Growing up in an African Caribbean household (my parents came from Jamaica to the UK in the late 1950s), I was exposed to hundreds of stories concerning the early years of their existence in this country.[2] Throughout the whole of my childhood, I was very much aware that people like my family and I were viewed as problems. We did not belong, and much that was said about us and done to us simply reinforced that view. One of the best books to have analysed that whole experience of marginalisation is Paul Gilroy's *There Ain't No Black in The Union Jack*.[3] Gilroy and others have demonstrated the extent to which negative attitudes to Black people and people of colour have been deeply embedded within the consciousness of this country.[4]

What has characterised Britain has been a deeply contradictory attitude to foreigners and those seeking entry into this country. In many respects, Britain has been, and to some extent remains, a bastion of democratic liberal values that enable it to welcome and become home to those seeking refuge and a safe hospitable space.[5] Yet, placed along-side this admirable tolerance and inclusivity, there has been a nasty whiff of xenophobia and racism directed towards those who are not deemed to be 'one of us'.[6]

The experience of Black and minority ethnic people in Britain has been one largely of struggle and hardship. Success has been fleeting and hard earned. What has sustained many of us has been the Christian faith, and a belief in the radical teachings of Jesus and the prophetic, liberating qualities of the Gospel.[7] When we face hardship, it is in the nature of Black Christians in particular to rally together, pray and confront our pain and sorrows head on, largely through the cultural repertoire of cooking food.[8] Our cultural contribution to this country has been immense and is a testament to the stakeholding we have invested in Britain over the past 50 or so years.

I hope that the following exercise will remind us all of the importance and value of each human being, irrespective of the labels society places on them. This is especially pertinent, given the seemingly endless column inches on the crisis in our procedures for dealing with asylum seekers. This apparent crisis sits alongside the biblical witness, where Jesus reminds us that one of the hallmarks of the Kingdom is that strangers are made welcome.[9]

The exercise is different to the other pieces in this book in that it is not a dramatic sketch or dialogue. Also, because it is dealing with an issue with which many in the Church are uncomfortable, I have been slightly more prescriptive than in the other pieces, by providing an accessible narrative/commentary for how the exercise can be 'unpacked' and reflected upon. As the reflections are written for young people in the first instance, some adults – particularly those who are familiar with the issues involved in this area of work – may find it a little simplistic. For these individuals, I simply encourage you to develop your own reflections to the exercise – ones which will be appropriate for the context in which you work and the groups with whom you normally engage.

Action

You will need to prepare a series of strips on which are written the phrases listed below. You will also require a long piece of string or rope – one which is long enough to stretch from one side of the room to the other. Alternatively, you can use a long broom-handle instead of the string or rope. You will need a large collection of sweets, chocolate etc. to act as prizes for the following exercise.

The following phrases should be written out and placed onto small strips of paper. You will need one strip per phrase:
• 'You are a 15-year-old Black/Asian male who has been excluded from school.'
• 'You are a 50-year-old White businessman.'

- 'You are a refugee who has just come to this country.'
- 'You are a school teacher.'
- 'You are a Black refugee in this country who cannot speak English.'
- 'You are a young Black/Asian person driving a large, expensive car.'
- 'You are an unemployed Black teenager with no qualifications.'
- 'You are a member of the Royal family.'
- 'You are an outspoken Black/Asian young person with a lot to say.'
- 'You are a Black person who is good at football.'
- 'You are a rich businessman.'
- 'You are a student at Oxford University.'
- 'You are a landlord who owns cheap property in which live poor Black people.'
- 'You are a Judge.'
- 'You are a Black person who has dreadlocks.'
- 'You are a Black/Asian person who is good at singing and dancing.'
- 'You are a Black/Asian person with a posh accent, who wears a pin-striped suit.'
- 'You are a poor White person from a large council estate.'
- 'You are a White immigration officer.'
- 'You are an elderly Asian shopkeeper.'
- 'You are a White police officer.'
- 'You are an elderly Black person who came to Britain in 1956.'
- 'You are a White bouncer on the door of a posh nightclub.'
- 'You are a White minister in a small church in the country.'

When you have prepared the strips with the various descriptions written on each one, ask the group of individuals to stand in a long line. Ask for two volunteers to hold the string/rope at either end, so that it is held out as far as it can stretch. (As the exercise takes place, you can ask different people to take it in turns to hold the string/rope at either end.) The two people holding the string/rope are asked to stand in the middle of the room. Explain the exercise to the individuals, which is as follows.

In the exercise, there are a number of strips of paper. On each is the description of a person. The person has a specific role, job or personality/characteristics. Each person has a particular value to this country. That value is worked out in the following way:

- How much power does this person have?

- Can they get things done?
- How important are they to the country as a whole and the people around them?
- Does the country see this person as being important?

You should place all the strips into a large tin and shuffle them. Ask each individual in the group to take a strip. Explain to the group that they have to decide, together as a whole group, how valuable each person is, according to the strip they have taken out of the tin. Remember the questions they have to take into account when making their decisions.

When the group has decided how valuable or important the person on a strip of paper is, they then have to set the height of the string/rope. The more valuable (or important) the person is, the higher will be the string/rope. Of course, the opposite is the case: if the person is not very valuable or important, the string/rope will be very low. In order for the exercise to work effectively, the group should be very strict about how high (or not) the string/rope should be. Obviously, if it needs to be very low, then they should not be afraid to make it that way.

Place the sweets, chocolate etc. on a table at the other side of the room. Inform the group that the various objects on the table are the prizes each individual will receive if they are able to cross the barrier that divides the room into two. If/when each individual is able to get to the other side of the room, overcoming the barrier in the middle, they can choose what prize from the table they would like to receive.

The exercise works as follows: Each person, in turn, collects a strip from the tin. They read out the words that are written on the strip. What type of person are they?

Next, the whole group must decide how valuable or important that person is. What is their value to the country? (See, above, the questions that should guide them.)

When the group has decided how valuable/important the person is, the whole group must then convert that importance and value into height. At what height should the string/rope be set? Remember that the more valuable/important the person is, the higher will be the string/rope. For some, the string/rope might be very, very low.

When the height has been set, the person who chose that strip has to attempt to move underneath the string/rope without touching it. If the person manages to get beneath the string/rope, they can go to the other side of the room and collect a prize from the table.

The aim of the game is to see how many of them are able to get under (it may mean crawling) the string/rope in order to gain a prize. Depending upon the person they have drawn from the strips, their task of attempting to gain a prize will either be fairly easy or very difficult. Some people are given a high value and are seen as important. Others are seen in the opposite way. Some people can gain a prize quite easily; others are not so fortunate.

When everyone has had a number of opportunities to attempt to gain a prize, ask the group to reflect upon the exercise:

- How many of them were able to gain a prize? Who managed to get under the string/rope?
- How did they decide on the value of each person?
- Which people were given the highest value? Why?
- What makes someone important or valuable?
- Which people were not seen as valuable or important?
- Which people had very little power to do things or make things happen?
- Which people were able to get to the other side and gain a prize?
- How did the various individuals feel about the people they chose?
- Who would have liked to win a prize but was unable to do so?
- Who was happy with the value given to the person they chose from the tin?
- What sorts of people were able to gain the prizes?

Reflection

In the exercise in which you have just taken part, every individual chose a particular person and was given a value, which made them important or not very important. The value or importance of each person was then converted into something that was real – i.e. the height of the string/rope. That conversion had a very real effect and impact upon each person in the group. Following on from the discussion, was the real task of trying to win the prize.

When individuals tried to win the prize, the true importance or significance of the value they had been given became obvious. If you were seen as important or valuable, you suddenly had a much better chance of overcoming the barrier or obstacle that lay in front of you. Some people had a great opportunity to win a prize; others were not given the same opportunity.

(Ask the group to reflect once again upon the people who were able to gain a prize and those who were not. What value or importance was given to each person?)

Clearly, from the exercise, we can see that certain people were seen as more important and valuable than others were, and these people usually won the prizes. Others may well have been able to win the prize, but they had to work harder, put in more effort and overcome greater hardships in order to win through.

(Do you think this is fair? Why were some people given more value and importance than others were?)

For over a thousand years, people in this country have been given a certain value and have been treated in a particular way depending upon how they have been seen. Over a thousand years ago, some people were noble people whilst others were servants or commoners. The latter were poor and had very few rights. It was decided that some people were better, more important and more valuable than others.

This form of placing particular value and importance upon some people became more dangerous when White Europeans began to travel the world in the middle part of the last millennium. When Europeans met people from the African continent and people from other parts of the world, they soon decided that these people were inferior to White people like themselves.[10] Certain very important people – some Church leaders (ministers and bishops), people in government and the royal family – decided that Black, Asian and Chinese people were inferior creatures who did not deserve to be given the same value or importance as White people like themselves. This type of prejudice led to countless examples of discrimination, which in turn led to widespread forms of racism.[11]

For hundreds of years, White Europeans used their belief in the inferiority of Black people, in particular, to create a very lucrative, money-making system called slavery. This system was one where Black people from Africa were captured and sold to White people in Britain, the Caribbean and the Americas in much the same way as you would sell a car or a horse or any other kind of object. Many Black people in Britain today, whose older relatives come from the Caribbean and the Americas, are descendants of these slaves who were taken in captivity from Africa to the so-called 'New World' of America and the Caribbean. These White Europeans were able to do this type of work quite easily and not feel very badly about it, because the Africans they captured were seen as barely human. The captured people were given less value or importance than that given to White Europeans.

(Think back to the value or importance you gave to every person. Why were certain people given more importance than others were? Who were seen as most valuable? Who was seen as the least important?)

In the exercise you played, the group first decided upon the value or the importance of each person. In many ways, you were doing exactly the same kind of thing that has been taking place in this country for hundreds, if not thousands of years. British societies have always seen some people as being more valuable than others. Just as you did in the exercise, so this country as a whole has chosen some people to be important whilst others have been overlooked or treated less well.

(What made the task of gaining the prize so difficult? Was it due only to what was said or thought about the person by the whole group? Was there some other reason that made getting the prize more difficult for some and easier for others?)

In the exercise, it was not only the words and thoughts of the whole group that made things difficult or easy. When the group talked about each person and then gave that person a value or a certain level of importance, that alone did not make their task of gaining the prize either easy or difficult. Of course, that discussion and the final decision were very important. What made the final task easy or difficult was the conversion of that decision into height in the exercise.

The prejudice that may have determined the value or importance of each person was then converted into something real, which then made the task of each person either easy or quite hard. That conversion in this country and in many other parts of the world is known as racism. Whilst prejudice is real, it is often elusive and hard to pin down. Racism, on the other hand, is often defined as 'prejudice + power'. The power bit is the ability to convert the prejudice (i.e. prejudging people on the basis of limited information, myths and half-truths) into something concrete, which then limits and has a concrete effect upon the person concerned. So in the exercise, the value given to each person was partly determined by the prejudices we *all* have as people, but it was not until that value was given a tangible, practical dimension (i.e. being turned into a height and an obstacle) that it then moved from being prejudice into being racism.

In the exercise, certain people were given more opportunity to overcome the obstacle or barrier in order to gain the prizes at the other side of the room. In Britain there are many prizes we can gain. What are some of the prizes we can gain in this country? (A nice house in a nice area. A good job. Good education. Money to buy things you would like to have. The freedom to travel. The freedom to come and go in this country when you choose. What about the right to come to this country in the first place?) Which people are denied the opportunity to gain some of the prizes?

(What are some of the ways in which racism prevents some people from gaining some of the prizes that are available in this country?)

Looking at contemporary Britain, we can see that there are many ways in which particular people are denied access to or opportunity to gain some of the prizes that are available in this country. For some, it is through unemployment. Black people are more likely to be unemployed than White people are. Similarly, a Black person is more likely to be stopped and searched by the police than a White person is. Sometimes, it is not what people do to you or against you that denies you the opportunity to gain the prize; it may be what people fail to do. Thousands of African and Asian people served this country bravely in two world wars, yet have been denied the opportunity to have their efforts rewarded and celebrated, because they have been overlooked. These people have not been able to gain the prize of being hailed as heroes, because of the racism that has overlooked or ignored their contributions and efforts.

This session has been called 'Stakeholding' because of the way in which all people, no matter what their differences may be, are in theory given the opportunity to stake a full claim to this country.

Look again at the words of the Universal Declaration of Human Rights (at the beginning of the opening reflections above). Is this declaration real for all people in Britain?

Racial justice is about the determination to see and treat all people equally, and give them the same rights and opportunities, no matter what 'race', ethnicity, cultures, religions or backgrounds they come from. It is about valuing and seeing all people as being equally important, whether they are like us, or are very different, in terms of their language, the clothes they wear, or their skin colour. As we can see from the exercise and the following reflections, this has rarely been the case for hundreds, if not thousands, of years. Racial injustice has been in existence for a very long time.

We are expected to value and see all people as being important. This is due not only to there being a Universal Declaration of Human Rights, or even a belief in fairness and equality. The most powerful reason for all people being treated with respect and being seen and treated with equal importance and value, is due to the fact that we are all created in God's image.

(Consider the biblical principles that govern our understanding of racial justice).[12]

Two key passages that confirm the importance of racial justice are:

> Malachi 2:10: 'Have we not all one Father, did not one God create us? Why do we profane the covenant [i.e. agreement or contract] of our fathers by breaking faith with one another?'

> Genesis 1:27: 'So God created man in his own image ... male and female he created them.'

So racial justice is not just a good idea, it is something that is at the very heart of God's concern for the world he has created. Jesus came that all people might have life and that life should be lived to the fullest. As we can see, not all people are given the opportunity to live life to the full.

But what can we do? The Racial Justice Sunday pack gives a number of clues as to what we can do, both as individuals and as groups of people.

(Ask the group to reflect for the final time upon the exercise and the following reflections. What can we do to bring about racial justice as it applies to us, or to people we know? How have we been affected? How can we support one another and other people?)

A final thought

'The little we attempt to do is never wasted, if we place it before God and ask for God's blessings upon our efforts. God can and will use our efforts to do mighty things.'

The Quest for Racial Justice

Opening reflections

The following extended dialogue was written originally for a presentation given by the Connexional Racial Justice Office to the Methodist Council a few years ago. My aim in writing this piece was to answer a number of anticipated questions that arise when one raises the issue of racial justice within predominantly church circles.

One of the strengths of using a dialogical approach to raising particular issues and concerns lies in the facility it offers the writer to adopt a range of voices (often imaginary) and perspectives in any dramatic piece.[1] Rather than speaking at people in a very direct way (which can sound very sermon-like or overly dictatorial), the writer can use different characters to express a range of views, which can enable the reader (or the actor) to become part of a conversation.

In using this dialogical structure, I hope to provide those who want to begin a journey into learning more about racial justice issues (with a view to going on further, using some of the resources developed by specialists in this area) with a safe, accessible starting point. I wanted this piece to counter some of the so-called common-sense ideas of racism and racial injustice that are often put forward by many 'right wing' publications such as some of our tabloid and broadsheet national newspapers.

The dialogue is relatively straightforward, and does not require any further explanation, save to say that on a practical note, because this is a long sketch for only two voices, you might want to divide the group into two. One group becomes No. 1 and the other No. 2. Then individuals from the two groups take it in turns to speak the lines alternately as written in the sketch.

———◄○►———

The Quest for Racial Justice

(A dialogue looking at issues of racial justice within the Church.)

NO. 1: *(To No. 2)* I was wondering if you could help me?

NO. 2: Yes, go on.

NO. 1: What's this I've been hearing about the need for racial justice in the Church? I read about it in some Church newspaper. Do you know anything about it?

NO. 2: Yeah, what do you want to know?

NO. 1: Well, this newspaper report says, and I quote: *(Pretending to read from a piece of paper)* 'Advocates for racial justice are asking the Church to address fundamental questions about our commitment to racial justice, about our identity and culture and how we shape the Church.'

NO. 2: And what you want to know is?

NO. 1: Well … *(Pause)* … What fundamental questions are we talking about?

NO. 2: Questions of equality, fairness, inclusiveness and justice. The exercising of power and authority in ways that promote the dignity and self-worth of all people within the Church and beyond it.

NO. 1: Equality and fairness? I thought the Church was full of equality and fairness. We are the Church, after all. We go in for that kind of thing. Speaking as a good Christian, I like a bit of fairness and equality like the next man … *(Correcting himself very quickly)* … woman … person … human being of non-specified gender. You know what I mean. We're all into fairness and equality these days. It's the trendy thing to do.

NO. 2: It may be the trendy thing to do. We may all talk the language of fairness and equality, but that doesn't mean that we practise it. Good intentions are all very well and good. But good intentions don't rectify issues of inequality and injustice. We need to go further. That's why racial justice advocates have been active over many years.

NO. 1: OK. So we have some fundamental questions to address. Questions related to fairness and equality.

NO. 2: Amongst others, which include developing Black leadership, Black participation in all areas and all levels in the Church, the teaching of Black Theology, racism awareness and more empowerment programmes for Black people.

NO. 1: Me and my big mouth! This report says some people feel they aren't being treated with fairness and equality. So who are these people?

NO. 2: Black people in the White-majority churches, for example.

NO. 1: Here we go again. More gripes and complaints. That's all we ever hear. What are they complaining about now?

NO. 2: I didn't suggest that 'they' were all complaining. And if you only ever hear the gripes, then maybe you need to ask yourself the question, what do they have to be unhappy about? In fact, I would say that the majority of Black people would rarely share their grievances and hurt, no matter how deep-seated and painful they may be.

NO. 1: Well, there you go, then. If people won't tell you what is going on, then how on earth are you expected to do anything about it?

NO. 2: What if you don't have the confidence to say what you feel?

NO. 1: Well, that's no fault of the Church. 'These' people should learn to speak up ... *(Very pretentious and patronising)* ... 'They' should be able to enunciate and articulate quite clearly ... *(Begins to raise his/her voice)* ... so that their voice can be heard.

NO. 2: I take your point. Could you do me a favour? *(No. 1 nods)* Will you answer this question for me? Why don't you eat pork?

NO. 1: Because it is against my principles and the cultural practices of my background.

NO. 2: But why don't you eat pork again?

NO. 1: Because it is contrary to my dietary habits. It is not in accordance with my own background.

NO. 2: But why don't you eat pork again?

NO. 1: I've just told you.

NO. 2: But why don't you eat pork again?

NO. 1: *(Beginning to get angry)* You're not listening to what I'm saying.

NO. 2: But why don't you eat pork again?

NO. 1: *(Angry)* This is pointless. You're wasting my time.

NO. 2: But why don't you eat pork again?

NO. 1: I'm not saying another word. This is stupid.

NO. 2: So why don't you eat pork again? ... *(Silence)* ... I'm sorry? Cat got your tongue? ... Touchy, aren't we? Imagine how you would feel if your attempts to raise your concerns were constantly misunderstood or fell on seemingly deaf ears. After a while you would become silent. And your silence might then be taken as assent and contentment.

NO. 1: I see what you mean. So how do you overcome that? How do you get people to continue sharing their experiences?

NO. 2: Through empowerment programmes. Giving people training and encouragement, so that they feel able to share what they are feeling and thinking and to keep on doing it until change finally comes about.

NO. 1: So this talk about fairness and equality is about helping people to speak their mind and have their voices heard?

NO. 2: In part, but there is more to it than that. Much more!

NO. 1: Such as?

NO. 2: It's also about affirming the importance of all people. Valuing and recognising their talents, gifts, skills and experiences. Helping all people to feel that their presence in the Church is invaluable to its ongoing life and mission.

NO. 1: But you're not telling me that we don't do that already? We're the Church! We're past masters of that. We taught the rest of the world all about that kind of stuff ... *(Pause)* ... Didn't we? Don't tell me I've got it wrong again?

NO. 2: Not entirely. The Church does attempt to value all people. The intentions are exceedingly good. But ...

NO. 1: The dreaded but ... Go on, what is it we don't do?

NO. 2: It's not so much what we don't do. It's more what we actually do. We attempt to value all people. It's just that we value some people as much more important than others. Let me ask you a question.

NO. 1: Not another question! Alright, I'm ready.

NO. 2: Describe to me the archetypal 'important' person in a historic White-majority church. The person who sits on the committees, goes to District Synods or their equivalent, attends annual national events or reads the denominational newspaper. Dare I say it? He or she actually reads the constitutional rule book and understands the Church's legislation.

NO. 1: You mean apart from some saddo, who wears thick Marks and Spencer's long check socks with shorts and sandles?

NO. 2: Apart from him.

NO. 1: Well. He's ... Well, he is more likely to be a he. He is well educated. Middle-aged and middle-class. Wears comfortable, sensible shoes, even sandals from time to time, along with the regulatory V-necked sweaters. Has more grey hair than the original of his youth. He is caring, considerate and invariably covenants to charity. He could be a lay person, but more often than not is a minister and has most likely been associated with the Church all his life.

NO. 2: Like most of the people in your average inner-city church? *(Slight pause)* ... Not! So the most 'important' and 'valuable' people are not usually unemployed, or Black, or women. Not usually what one might term working-class or from the underclass. Not necessarily someone who hates sensible shoes or recoils at the idea of putting on Marks and Spencer's knitwear! Not usually a newcomer to the church. Not usually someone to whom the idea of being a 'typical churchgoer' has been informed by cultures and practices that originated in hitherto mission fields such as Africa and the Caribbean, rather than by centuries of Anglo-Saxon mythology.

NO. 1: Come to think of it, the established Church in England does sometimes remind me of a glass of Guinness. The froth at the top is always White and the rest of the glass is Black.

NO. 2: There's nothing like a good alcohol-inspired metaphor. But I get what you mean. What we need is better representation at all levels of the Church. Black and minority ethnic people need to be seen at every level of the Church. Their skills, expertise and different experiences need to be affirmed. We need to value and affirm the importance of all varieties of people within the Church.

NO. 1: And the work of racial justice advocates is concerned with this?

NO. 2: Yes.

NO. 1: This quest for fairness and equality. What other forms does it take?

NO. 2: Well, imagine that one day I came to your house, broke down your front door and dragged you from your home. Ill treated you and kept you a prisoner in the house of another person. I denied you your liberty and deprived you of your property. I prevented you from remembering your previous life and experiences from the time when you lived in your own home. I also told you that your life was worth nothing and was not as valuable as mine. Now, supposing I did all this to you. Tell me, how would you feel?

NO. 1: You and your questions ... Well, I suppose I would feel angry.

NO. 2: Angry at whom?

NO. 1: You, of course.

NO. 2: Would you see God in the same way as I do?

NO. 1: Maybe not. There's no way I could believe that God wanted what had happened to me to continue. Surely God is against injustice?

NO. 2: For many Black people, historically, their experience can be likened to the figurative example I've just given. For the Church to be actively on the side of those who have been the victims of injustice, we need to hear the voices of the oppressed. We need to hear their experiences of God. How God sustains and empowers them through all their difficulties. We need to hear and understand how those experiences have underpinned their talk of God.

NO. 1: I agree.

NO. 2: Well, we need to promote and champion the cause of Black Theology, then.

NO. 1: Now, I don't know about that.

NO. 2: You just said that you agreed. Black Theology is a theology arising out of the struggles and the experiences of Black people over the past five centuries. Failure to appreciate and understand this is a failure to appreciate and understand the vitality and the very nature of Black people themselves.

NO. 1: Yes, I hear what you're saying. But I'm not comfortable with the idea of putting a term like 'Black' in front of a nice neutral term like 'theology'.

NO. 2: So you believe that a nice neutral term like 'theology' implies that the way in which we do theology is neutral?

NO. 1: Of course theology is neutral.

NO. 2: And people don't bring their human understanding and interpretations to bear upon Scripture?

NO. 1: No.

NO. 2: So when White Europeans used their theological understanding to assert the sub-human nature and the inferiority of Black people, even as recently as the 1960s and early 1970s, they were doing what? So the Bible actually sanctions the oppression of some people? Or are you saying that advocates of Black Theology have been getting it wrong all these years?

NO. 1: Well, errm ... yeah ... I think I see ... sort of.

NO. 2: Acknowledging the importance of Black Theology is to recognise the legitimacy of other voices that come from different perspectives, and to affirm their talk of God in the light of their experiences. If we refuse to acknowledge these voices and experiences, then at what price can we talk about fairness and equality?

NO. 1: OK. I see your point. So racial justice has as one of its central concerns, a desire to promote fairness and equality for all people.

NO. 2: Yes, through strategies that challenge and seek to combat racism within the Church and in the wider society. There are courses in Racism Awareness for predominantly White people so that they can be sensitised to the issues of racism within the Church and society. There are other programmes related to Black Consciousness Raising, in addition to advice, training, consultancy and advocacy within the ongoing life of the Church.

NO. 1: So all of what you've just said is a part of your commitment to racial justice?

NO. 2: Yes, and many other important initiatives as well. Strategies such as ethnic monitoring, for example – knowing how many Black people we have in the Church and at what levels they are represented and involved in its life. Ignorance can build resentment. Ignorance is never bliss – it's simply a bad position to be in. So we need to eradicate any lingering examples of ignorance.

NO. 1: By teaching Black Theology in our theological colleges, I suppose?

NO. 2: Yes, plus other courses to empower and instil confidence in Black members within the Church.

NO. 1: What else?

NO. 2: Creating the necessary space for Black people to meet by themselves to discuss issues that are of special and unique concern to them. This needs to be done without the sometimes inhibiting presence of White people in attendance, who may curtail or limit certain discussions from taking place. Often, Black people are inhibited in saying what they really feel in front of White people, for fear of offending them. So they often submerge their real feelings and experiences. That's why they sometimes need to meet separately from White people.

NO. 1: Now, I don't know if I agree with that. That sounds very divisive to me. It even has the whiff of *apartheid*, or reverse discrimination, even.

NO. 2: But it's a recognised strategy that marginalised groups should be encouraged on particular occasions to meet separately. We have groups for women, groups for young people, groups for people who are Gay and Lesbian. Black people have the right to meet by themselves for the purposes of support, affirmation, self-confidence and to discuss particular issues that have a distinct impact upon their lives. Black people don't want to leave or become members of some breakaway church. They want to be members of their own churches, like everyone else. Valued and affirmed for the contribution they can make to the life of the Church.

NO. 1: It still sounds unhealthy to me.

NO. 2: If the Church is serious about promoting the cause of racial justice, then we have to understand that there will need to be occasions when those who have been oppressed and treated unfairly are given the space to articulate their feelings and experiences in an environment that is affirming and non-judgemental. Trust me, it really can be difficult if White people are present.

NO. 1: I still don't like the idea of that.

NO. 2: With all due respect, you would say that, wouldn't you? This is not about you; it is about the bigger cause of racial justice within the Church. It is also about the Church having a prophetic voice to challenge the wider society as a whole. In many cases, it has been opportunities to meet together in this kind of setting that have enabled Black people to remain in the Church. So you have a choice, my friend. Either Black people meet together and empower one another in order that they can remain, or you deny them such opportunities and they decide to leave the Church altogether. Then what happens? Have a guess?

NO. 1: I don't know ...

NO. 2: We have no inner-city churches. The churches' presence in inner-city areas comes to an end. It is the presence of Black people that is keeping many of these churches open. So you see, racial justice even has a practical, pragmatic, self-interest angle to it.

NO. 1: All this sounds like a really complicated piece of business to me.

NO. 2: It is, for all of us – both Black and White! It is a long, painful and very costly process. Costly in terms of money, time and resources. It is also costly in terms of the pain and alienation felt by many of our young Black people who feel marginalised from our churches.

NO. 1: This is far more important than I had imagined. There is a great deal at stake.

NO. 2: But if we are to move beyond good intentions towards actuality, then the pain and cost will have to be endured and owned by all within the Church, if we are to be truly one Church. Racial justice is an issue for both Black and White people. When Black people are affirmed and empowered, that has a knock-on effect for the whole Church. When the marginalised and the dispossessed are able to play a meaningful part in the Church, then the whole Church benefits.

NO. 1: We are our brother's … *(Slight pause)* … and sister's keeper.

NO. 2: And all are children of God, all are created in God's image and all are equal.

NO. 1 & NO. 2: Amen!

THE END

---◄○►---

Post-sketch reflections

For a variety of reasons that are not too difficult to fathom, this dialogue has been one of the least used amongst the collection of work that comprises this book. On the occasions when it has been used, it has elicited a great deal of debate amongst all participants. Those discussions have been very informative and helpful, but they have been limited, due to the inability of the participants to 'enter into' the creative space of the 'other'. By using this phrase, I am talking about the overarching difficulty of trying to get beyond the fragile and insecure subjectivity we all carry when dealing with issues of 'race'.

The tensions regarding issues of 'race' are all too evident in much of our contemporary discourse, whether inside or outside the Church. To quote Richard Reddie (and yes, he is my brother, before you ask): 'The Church often avoids race-related discussions through fear, ignorance and a sense of seeming irrelevance.'[2]

The central defining metaphor of being the united body in Christ makes many Christians unable or unwilling to deal with issues of difference and the racism that arises from our refusal to often engage with or even acknowledge that reality which separates and divides us. Writing with reference to the Eucharist, Tee Garlington reminds us of the ethnic tensions, and the inherent inclusivity that should embrace these differences, both of which reside within Jewish and Christian traditions.[3] Garlington continues, reminding us that the early Church had to struggle with issues of racial or national intolerance, but the praxis (the action or activity) of those first Christians sought to move beyond those racial issues.[4]

The tensions that have arisen when this sketch has been performed and then reflected upon are reminders that the ongoing phenomenon of racism is one that holds many of us hostage. Enoch Oglesby has employed the metaphor of the mountain in his attempt to makes sense of and grapple with the often unnamed and unspoken sin that is racism.[5] Oglesby attempts to use Christian ethics to challenge the reality of racism in the US. He argues that the Black church in America has become absorbed into a White-middle-class form of complacency that wants to ignore the reality of racism and identify it as someone else's problem – that is, secular society's problem. Oglesby writes:

> Thus, Black folk are faced, in this regard, with a double-barrelled moral dilemma: the sinful scandal of racism within the comfortable pews of the church, on the one hand; and on the other, the immorality of bourgeois power arising from the church's uncritical identification with the dominant class values of the status quo.[6]

The challenge for all us, the united and yet diverse body of Christ, is to find ways of being open about our differences (as well as those things which unite us) and to name the sin that corrupts our sense of corporate unity. This dialogue (admittedly, much too wordy and long-winded) has proved useful, in that it is an amalgam of every conversation I have had when trying to discuss racism with White people. The reason for its wordy format was due to my intention to 'second guess' every attempt at 'British reasonableness',[7] which tries to challenge anti-racist or racial justice polemics by 'picking holes' or constructing pedantic 'commonsense' arguments. I wonder whether we will ever get to a place where racism can be discussed dispassionately and with equal commitment by both Black and White?

Follow-up questions

Read Luke 10:25–37 and reflect upon the dialogue you have just read or performed.

- In the passage, the Samaritan goes beyond his own cultural boundaries to support and care for another person. How can your church take similar action?
- How do you think the Samaritan fits into this sketch? What would he do?
- The dialogue is very much concerned with Black people in White-majority churches. How might this scenario be 'played out' or expressed in a Black-majority church setting? What are the hidden or submerged examples of internalised racism in these settings?
- What does the passage have to say to both characters in the dialogue?
- What points raised in the dialogue made an impression upon you? (And why?)
- Quite often, raising racial justice issues can make many of us feel uncomfortable. Reflecting upon the dialogue, how can we create the kind of environment that allows us to discuss these issues in an honest and supportive way?
- How do you feel about Black church members on occasions meeting separately from their White brothers and sisters in Christ? Is the reason given for this in the dialogue a plausible one for you? (If yes, then why? If no, then why not?)
- What can you do to help forward the cause of racial justice
    (a) within your personal discipleship,
    (b) within your church and
    (c) further afield?

Black Voices

Opening reflections

In an earlier piece I outlined an approach to re-setting and interpreting the Bible from a Black Jamaican/African Caribbean context.[1] In that dramatic reading, I commented on some of the negative aspects of Black cultural values and life. In this piece, I want to take this issue even further, by looking at the different positions and values adopted by various people within Diasporan Black British communities. I have sought to do this by way of constructing a fictional social gathering – a party, or in Black speak, a 'dance', at which a variety of people and voices are present.

One of the challenges facing Black theologians and cultural commentators is the necessity to develop a more honest and holistic view of Black cultures and the practices that exist within various Black communities. Too often, Black scholars (myself included) have concentrated our efforts (quite rightly, for the most part) on the external challenges that have confronted us, such as racism, for example, with less emphasis being given to the internal issues and struggles that exist within our own communities.

For example, when seeking to describe and illustrate Black community living, great emphasis has been placed on the examples of solidarity and community. The many examples of homogeneity or sameness have been highlighted. This is particularly the case when scholars have spoken about Black and Black-majority churches.[2] Our tendency to view Black communities as monolithic has meant that the diverse range of experiences and values that exist within the overall whole tends to be either downplayed or ignored altogether. I have addressed some aspects of this tendency to mythologise or romanticise aspects of Black culture in my previous book.[3]

On occasions, there is a type of hierarchy of 'Blackness' in Black communities, where some people are judged as belonging in a more complete fashion than others. There are many Black people who have been accused of not 'really being Black' or not being 'Black enough'.[4] Scholars such as Michael Eric Dyson,[5] Kobena Mercer[6] and most notably, Victor Anderson[7] have challenged us to see beyond the often strait-jacketed interpretations we place on Black cultural expression and lived experience. Anderson, in particular, has challenged the way in which Black religious, cultural critics have wanted to acknowledge only the 'positive aspects' of Black life, and have often sought to overlook or ignore those elements of which we are not so proud.[8] As Anderson reminds us, we cannot all be saints, heroes and 'trailblazers'.

Similarly, within the biblical witness, there are as many flawed ex-amples of humanity and 'fallenness', through which God's redemptive work is done, as there are so-called heroes and those of supposedly blameless character – King David is an obvious candidate that springs to mind in terms of the former. Michael Eric Dyson's honest account of the life of Martin Luther King is an important example of dealing with the wholeness of human experience, and not just the edited highlights.[9]

In a later book, the same author attempts a critical reassessment of the life of the deceased rapper, Tupac Shakur. Dyson opens up new possibilities for us to see beyond the limitations of 'heroes' and 'villians', 'good people' and 'bad' ones.[10] Life, culture and cultural expression are complex and often contradictory. I have consciously sought to create a series of stereotypes in this sketch. I make no apologies for this, for I sense that beneath many stereotypes there usually resides an element (albeit relatively small) of truth. All these characters exist within the many Black communities of Britain. We all know some, if not all, of these people. Some will be familiar to us and we may possess affinity or fond feelings for them. In the case of others, the opposite will be the case. Without wishing to be overly pious or sanctimonious, that is exactly the point. The challenge of this sketch is to confront and acknowledge all these characters head on. Who are they and why do they act the way they do?

In writing *Black Voices* I wanted to find a way of illustrating the whole range of Black expression that may exist in any particular setting. Can we legitimately say that church is an expression of the Kingdom, when only certain kinds of people are permitted to attend, and be heard? How does our notion of 'being church' then compare with Jesus' inclusive instructions for those attending the wedding feast in Luke chapter 14? Are we guilty of being more prescriptive and concerned with correctness and acceptability than was Jesus – a man who kept company with prostitutes, tax collectors and other socially 'undesirable' people? Who do we consider to be part of 'us', and who should not belong?

———◄○►———

Black Voices

(The scene ... we see a bar. A tall man is standing nonchalantly behind the bar [a table with a few drinks on it]. We are inside a house at a family party. We see two people at the bar – a man and a woman. They are arguing.)

MABEL: Me noh know why me ever marry such a' wort'less piece a' man like yu ... See yu ... *(Kisses her teeth)* ...

BARMAN: *(Polite)* Can I serve either one of you?

LAWRENCE & MABEL: *(In unison)* Shut up!

LAWRENCE: *(Raising his hand to fight)* No bodder wrenk wi mi 'oman. If yu mek I raise fe my left han' an' clap yu t'ree kin' a' lik' cross yu neck back, yu go'n filt yu foot.

MABEL: *(Boxes Lawrence)* Who yu go'n box hi? Mi? Yu tek mi fe fool ... *(Boxes him again)* ... Tek de lik, yu no shame, bruck-down, mash-up piece a' man.

(Barman attempts to intervene.)

BARMAN: Could I be of help here?

LAWRENCE & MABEL: *(In unison)* Shut up!

MABEL: Now me go'n ax yu again ... *(Looking around)* ... Wey she dey?

LAWRENCE: *(Half-hearted and pathetic)* Me noh know wha' yu a' talk 'bout.

MABEL: *(Slaps Lawrence again)* Noh lie to me ... Wey de man, tiefing Jezebel? Me wan' drop three kin' a' lik innah she face. No one go'n tief my man, yu hear mi?

(Mabel slaps Lawrence one last time.)

LAWRENCE: *(Head bowed, totally defeated)* Yes, dear ... *(Mutters under his breath)* ... Diam miserable wretch.

MABEL: *(To Lawrence)* Wha' dat? Yu 'ave somet'ing fi sey? *(Lawrence shakes his head slowly ... Mabel looks into the distance and sees someone coming. It is Janet)* ... A' she?

(Enter Janet.)

JANET: Hello, Lawrence.

MABEL: *(Leaps at Janet and grabs her around the throat)* Tek yu han' off my man ... Mi noh go'n warn yu again.

JANET: *(Shaking Mabel's hands off her neck)* I don't know what you're talking about.

MABEL: Noh lie to me. If dere's one t'ing mi cyan 'tan, and dat's a' laired ...

LAWRENCE: 'Top yu noise, 'oman. Wha mek yu so miserable?

MABEL: *(Boxes her husband again ... She leaps at Janet again)* Now mi go'n warn yu fi de las' time ... Tek yu han' off fe me man.

JANET: *(Breaks Mabel's hold ... Angry)* Look! I don't know who you think you are. No one talks to me like that! Do you think I would be stupid enough to deal with an ugly, disgusting-looking man like that? ... *(Points to Lawrence's bedraggled and pathetic figure)* ... Look at him. Don't make me laugh. That man is nasty.

MABEL: *(Thinking for a moment)* Alright den. 'Im nasty fi true ...

(Exit Mabel. There is a short interval as Janet and Lawrence pretend not to notice each other ... Then suddenly they leap into each other's arms. They begin to hug.)

BOTH OF THEM: Darling!

BARMAN: *(Inquiring)* Can I help either of you two?

LAWRENCE & JANET: *(In unison)* Shut up!

LAWRENCE: *(Standing back and looking at Janet)* Bwoy, yu look criss ... Mi love yu, yu know.

JANET: But what about your wife? She knows about us?

LAWRENCE: Cho! Dat hugly 'oman? Mi noh care 'bout ar ... She too diam fuhfool and chupid.

(The two of them begin to hug again. Enter Giles. Lawrence and Janet quickly break off their clinch. Giles approaches the bar. As he arrives, Mabel calls Lawrence off stage.)

MABEL: *(Off stage)* Lawrence! Tek yu frownsey cack off, broad batty over yahso ... *(Slight pause)* ... NOW!

LAWRENCE: *(Beginning to walk away, says to Janet:)* Mi mus' go, darling ... De dragon 'oman a' call mi ... Soon come.

(Exit Lawrence … Giles stands next to Janet … The Barman is peering at the two of them.)

GILES: *(Posh Etonian accent)* Hello! I was wondering if you could possibly help me?

BARMAN: *(Intervening eagerly)* I could help … I'm a barman. I'm trained to help people.

GILES: *(To the Barman)* Now, now, my good man, I was talking to the lady. I make it a point never to converse with the hired help. Now run along, my good man, and see if you can improve your education so that you can get a proper job … *(To Janet)* I'm a little lost. Well, terribly lost, actually. Is this the Henley-on-Thames Rotary Club?

JANET: What?

GILES: The Henley-on-Thames Rotary Club.

JANET: No.

GILES: Oh, dash it … I knew I should have taken the fifth exit on the motorway … But when one is doing 150 miles per hour in a 1962 Aston Martin Lagonda – silver bullet, complete with eight litres, overhead cam, leather-upholstered seats, aerodynamic foil, turbo boost, and sub-sonic road tracking – one finds it rather perturbing to have to break the flow, change down through my six co-ordinated, hydraulic, air-pressurised gears, and exit the motorway. I guess you find it quite perturbing as well?

JANET: What are you saying?

BARMAN: *(Intervening eagerly again)* I know what he's saying. I'll translate for you. I speak fluent Upper-Class Twit.

JANET & GILES: *(In unison)* Shut up!

GILES: *(To Janet)* Did you attend the Queen's garden party this year? I think I met you. Are you related to Lord Rothermere?

JANET: Are you for real, or are you pretending to be a stiff idiot?

GILES: My dear … I'm afraid I cannot divine the nature of your last remark. Are you calling into question the authenticity of my persona?

JANET: You're a stiff idiot for real. I've seen some big-faced, no-sense, small-brain idiots in my life. Men who are practised jack-asses. But you! You have a Ph.D. in stupidity. I feel sorry for you.

GILES: *(Pause)* Oh! I have tickets to Wimbledon next year. Would you care to mash it up in a different style with I, man?

JANET: *(Kisses her teeth)* Idiot.

(Enter a young ragga-ish youth. Walks with a pronounced swagger. Walks up to Giles and Janet at the bar.)

BIG BWOY: *(To Giles)* Yo my main man. Shed some skin ... *(Holds out a hand in order to exchange the customary greetings with Giles, but Giles is non-plussed.)* My man, Big Bwoy is the name, and cool runnings is my game. So what ya saying, Bro?

GILES: I wasn't aware one was required to engage in a dual discourse, in the form of a dialogue.

BIG BWOY: Come again, Bro?

BARMAN: *(Still eager)* I know what he's talking about. Please let me say something. Please, go on, please ... Let me, let me ... go on.

THE OTHER THREE: *(In unison)* Shut up!

GILES: Does one know the way to Hampton Court? Lord de Grenville is holding a coming-out party for his daughter ... Lucinda Perringrow. I'm hoping to attend. One should come along ... It will be absolutely spiffing.

BIG BWOY: *(Non-plussed)* Rewind and come again, selector. I don't understand the lyrics, Bro ... You're chatting foolishness. Pure foolishness ... You ain't no Black man. You're pure Bounty. A real coconut. Black on the outside, White as chalk on the inside. Runwey man, runwey.

(Big Bwoy chases Giles out of the scene ... he turns to talk with Janet.)

BIG BWOY: *(To Janet)* Wha'appen, Gorgeous ... You're sweet and nice. Like ice cream ... I could eat you up.

JANET: Get lost, creep.

BIG BWOY: Yo, sweet thing, don't do me like that. I've been waiting all my life for a woman like you. So what do you say, sweet thing? You and me? Mono on mono?

JANET: For such a bony, pigeon-chested wretch, you sure have a big ego.

BIG BWOY: *(Offended ... Exaggerated shock)* What yu saying, Sis? You trying to diss me? Me ... Big Bwoy? ... *(Begins to circle her)* ... Big Bwoy? Biggest and the baddest of all the bad men in town? What ya saying Sis, what you saying?

JANET: Look here, sparrow-chest ... If you didn't speak out of your bottom so much, your breath wouldn't smell so bad. At least your name is accurate. You are a boy ... *(Looking him up and down)* ... Only you're not very big, are you?

BIG BWOY: *(Furious)* What? What? Yu t'ink yu too nice or somet'ing? I should give you a taste of the back of my hand, sister ...

(Big Bwoy raises his fist to hit Janet ... Suddenly there is a loud voice off stage.)

LUTICIA: *(Shouting out)* Cuthbert ... Cuthbert ... Is that you?

BIG BWOY: *(Recoils in shame ... Puts his hands to his head)* Shame ... Big shame ...

(Enter Luticia ... exit Janet at the opposite end. Luticia approaches Big Bwoy.)

LUTICIA: *(To Big Bwoy)* Cuthbert ... Why don't you come when I call you?

BIG BWOY: *(Looking around)* Mum ... Do you have to? You know all my friends call me Big Bwoy.

LUTICIA: Well, I christen you Cuthbert, and dat is how you is going to stay ... *(Approaches Big Bwoy. Begins to look behind his ears and at the collar on his shirt.)* You remember to wash behind your ears before you come out? And look 'pon your shirt-collar? Pure nastiness. And did you change your brief this morning?

BIG BWOY: Clean underpants, Ma? Give it a rest.

BARMAN: *(Leaning across eagerly)* I changed my underpants this morning. Look, I'll show you.

(The Barman comes from behind the bar and begins to unzip his trousers.)

LUTICIA: *(Slaps him quickly)* Behave yourself, you blasted fool. What yu mek you t'ink I want to see your dutty brief?

BARMAN: *(Going back behind the bar)* But I thought ...

BIG BWOY & LUTICIA: *(In unison)* Shut up!

LUTICIA: *(To Big Bwoy)* What would happen if you get knock down by a train tomorrow? ... You want me to feel shame? And what about your socks? I can smell dem from here. And look 'pon you head. Not even Vaseline find itself in there ... And look 'pon you face. Not even cream. Bwoy you have no shame. You need some good old-fashion lick. Some bush lick ... *(Begins to open her handbag)* ... Me have a piece a belt in here somewhere. Bwoy, you need some beating. You is not too old fe get lash, you know.

(Big Bwoy runs off stage ... Luticia calls after him.)

LUTICIA: Cuthbert, where you going? Me talking to you. Cuthbert! Come back here now! ... Dat bwoy! He need some bush lick, me tell you. Some good old-fashion lashing. When my mother used to beat me, lard, me couldn't walk, let alone sit fi three days ... Dem English pickney get it easy, you know.

(Luticia storms off stage ... All is silent, save the Barman. He walks out from behind the bar and to centre stage, a big smile on his face.)

BARMAN: At last. My turn to talk. I've been dying to say something all night ... So where shall I start? What can I say? Well, I could tell you about the time I met Bob Marley. I taught him how to play guitar, you know. In actual fact, I don't want to boast, but I wrote 'Jamming' for him ... *(Begins to sing)* 'Jamming, I'm jamming, and I hope you like jamming too. Yeah, I'm jamming ...'

(Suddenly across the stage runs Janet, followed by Lawrence, who in turn is being chased by Mabel. All three stop momentarily to look at the Barman.)

ALL THREE: *(In unison)* Shut up!

LAWRENCE: *(To Janet)* Run, darling. De mad 'oman go'n kill de both a' we!

JANET: *(Begins to run again)* I'm running, I'm running!

MABEL: *(Also running now)* Yu can run, but yu cyan hide! An' when mi ketch de two a' yu ... Bwoy, yu betta run!

(Exit all three. The Barman is about to speak again. He steps forward when, across the stage, runs Big Bwoy followed by Luticia.)

BIG BWOY & LUTICIA: *(Both stop and look at the Barman)* Shut up!

BIG BWOY: *(Continues to run)* I can't stop, Ma ... You're ruining my credibility. Big Bwoy is too cool to take any kind a' shame.

LUTICIA: *(Continues to run also)* Cuthbert ... Cuthbert ... You remember to wash you cheesy feet? And you remember to put on your vest? You know how you easy fi catch cold?

(Exit Big Bwoy and Luticia ... The Barman is about to speak again, when Giles enters the scene.)

GILES: *(To Barman)* Oh, be quiet and run away, my ignorant friend ... *(To the audience)* ... Does anyone know the way to Buckingham Palace? Prince Charles and I are going to a Buju Banton concert ... We are going to pick up some patties along the way ... Charles does so like to niam. I'm partial to a bit of curried goat myself. Anyway, I must dash.

(Exit Giles ... The Barman finally walks forward to talk.)

BARMAN: At last ... As I was saying, I used to write songs for Bob Marley. We used to ...

(Enter all the other characters, who walk in front of the Barman and shout:)

EVERYONE EXCEPT BARMAN: Shut up!

BARMAN: *(Very sad)* Alright then!

THE END

———◄◌►———

Post-sketch reflections

One of the most obvious points that arise from a sketch such as this one is the fact that reactions to it are so clearly determined by the ethnicity or cultural location of the individual concerned. In the first instance, there is the sheer subject matter and identification with the characters concerned. Unlike many of the other pieces in this book (except *It Could Have Happened Like This*), the characters in *Black Voices* are not generic people. The ethnicity of the people in this sketch is key to its composition, hence the rather unsubtle title of *Black Voices*. The reactions to this sketch, therefore, have varied greatly depending upon the composition of the group engaging with it.

On the basis of my interaction with others in using this sketch, I would suggest that there have been two overarching categories of responses. First, when the groups have been monocultural, the reactions have differed, depending upon whether that group is a Black one or is comprised of White people. In terms of the latter, it has struck me that group participants have felt somewhat uneasy with the whole scenario. This is due in part to the cultural dislocation felt by many White people when exposed to self-consciously Black contexts.

Even within many Western societies, where many contexts (especially inner-city ones) are much more plural than they once were, it is still true that Black people know far more about White people and their cultural world, than is the reverse. Many of the White people (particularly if they were older) knew relatively little about the cultural world which many Black people inhabit. A number of scholars have commented on the difficulty experienced by many White people in their attempts to engage meaningfully with Black people.[11] This lack of awareness has led many of the White participants to struggle when trying to respond in any meaningful way to the characters in the sketch.

Another important issue is that of language. Many of the characters speak in a variety of linguistic forms that are reflective of African Caribbean cultures and are an important signifier of their sense of identity. Scholars such as Willis,[12] Tomlin[13] and Challoner[14] have all explored the importance of Black idioms to the identity construction of African Caribbean people in Britain. The linguistic traits of African Caribbean people are hugely important for the distancing effect they have exerted on White people. Basically, if people cannot follow what you are saying, then it becomes easier to sustain one's own self-determined identity, and to a lesser extent, one's destiny.[15]

The reaction amongst White-only groups is decidedly less marked when younger White people are involved. One of the clear effects of postmodernism is the realisation that many cultural boundaries have been exploded, with young people being able to cross many different barriers.[16] I have noted the extent to which younger White people have expressed greater facility to engage with the Black characters in the sketch.

Amongst Black-only groups the reaction to the sketch has been just as marked as that of White-only groups. For the Black participants, they have enjoyed being able to engage with this humorous and stereotypical sketch, which is very much reflective of the African Caribbean comic material of many contemporary Black comedians in the UK.[17]

The gusto and exuberant manner with which many Black people have engaged with this sketch reminds one of the importance of Black religio-cultural settings, particularly the Church, where Black identity and expression are given free rein. Robert Beckford's work, in particular, has been most notable for its critical assertion that the Black church in the UK is essential for providing a radical space in which Black selfhood can flourish.[18]

Black Voices has become for many a comedic template for what is the best and the worst of Black Christian expression. The strict moral climate of many Black churches is such that there appears to be a distinct chasm between those who are righteous (and saved) and those who are not.[19] It is a form of Christianity that rigidly adheres to a 'them and us' paradigm, which clearly makes judgements on the worthiness of particular people. *Black Voices* offers a useful framework for investigating the theology and practice of Black Christian contexts. For White people, this sketch challenges such individuals to reflect on how they relate to Black people, especially when they are in specific African and Caribbean contexts. How can we be brothers and sisters in Christ when there is limited or even no knowledge of the 'other'?

Follow-up questions

Read Luke 14:7–14.

- What challenge does the Gospel reading from Luke provide in our interpretation of this sketch and the people in it?
- Reflecting upon the sketch and the passage, which of the people in the sketch would you like to have at a party you were giving, and why? (Which people would you not invite or rather they did not attend?)
- What are the characteristics of a person who is truly 'Black'? (Why and on what information or values do you make your reflections?)
- Is the above question a legitimate one? If not, then why not? (Is there an answer?)
- Construct a list of the people in the sketch in terms of their value and the ways in which they represent Black people. Who is at the top, and who is at the bottom? (And why?)
- If you were at that party, what would you say to the different characters, in light of the passage?

ETHICS / ACTION

'If Christianity were simply about loving an invisible God, then life would be so easy.' I remember saying these words to a group of friends at a Methodist Society (Meth.Soc.) fellowship group meeting many years ago, when I was a student at the University of Birmingham. I was struck by the thought that what made life difficult as a Christian was not the metaphysical or supernatural elements of it all – the reality of God, Jesus rising from the dead or the presence of the Holy Spirit in our lives. For me, all that was child's play. What was hard, was the second of the great commandments of Jesus – loving your neighbour as yourself. Loving a God who is invisible and can be silent for very long periods can be quite easy. Loving your neighbour whom you can see, and who may make serious demands upon you, is a much harder proposition.

As a Black person who was born in this country and has lived here all my life, I have been aware of the continuing contradictions in the practice of Christianity in this country. I have seen people love God with all their heart, mind, soul and strength, and then, in their next breath, casually discriminate against their neighbour. I have witnessed good Christian people say one thing and most definitely and self-consciously do another, without even the merest hint of irony as they did so.

This can be seen in the church that, having read the parable of the Good Samaritan, then conveniently makes a rather pungent homeless person definitely unwelcome. Or the fellowship that closes its ranks to those who 'are not our sort of people'. In both contexts, the Church stands accused of perverting the Gospel of Christ. My commitment to Black and Liberation theologies has arisen from this experience of always being on the sharp end of such contradictions. As I have stated on a previous occasion, no one ever intended, intentionally, to discriminate, but they usually found a convenient way of doing so.[1]

In a conversation with an ex-student at the Queens Foundation, where I work, I was challenged to give further thought to a phenomenon that I had termed 'A Theology of Good Intentions'. This phrase and concept had arisen from a previous piece of research and was detailed in my last book.[2] The student wondered whether I should find a positive title or phrase that would act as an antidote to the negativity of the term I had coined. The conversation was a challenging one. It forced me to think further upon how theology and the Christian faith can construct resources that will enable us to better link the theory that guides us with the practice that will inspire others.

In creating the following pieces for this section of the book, I have begun to work on a new concept as a counter to 'A Theology of Good Intentions'. The title for this new term is tentatively named as 'A Theology of Dramatic Engagement'.[3] In using this term, what I want to suggest is that the primary way in which Christian understanding or action has developed, has not been through further in-depth study or thinking. It has not been through prolonged reflection and discussion. Although these elements are undoubtedly important, it is my belief that change occurs through active participation with others, especially those who are not like us.[4]

The previous section on racial justice offers us, I believe, a useful case in point. From the accounts of older Black people living in Britain,[5] I have come to understand how a so-called Christian nation such as this one became adept at discriminating and displaying marked examples of prejudice resulting in racism towards those who were not White. The changes in attitudes over the past half century, since the bulk of African and Caribbean peoples landed on these shores, have arisen not through extended intellectual thought. One might even argue, what was there to think about? There is no sustainable justification for racism within the Scriptures.[6] Surely, we should have been treating our neighbours as ourselves all along?

What has prompted societal and attitudinal changes has been the necessity, indeed the need, to engage with one another. In church contexts, for example, when the 'White flight' of the middle class meant that formerly White-majority churches suddenly became Black-majority ones, people had to learn to engage. That practical engagement, when infused with the prevenient spirit of creativity, has given rise to new forms of practical theology, which in turn, has led to discernible change.

'A Theology of Dramatic Engagement' has been in existence for as long as Christian people have been forced to deal with the realities of life. It has used the historic resources of Scripture, a re-interpretation of tradition, reason and human experience to find new ways of living with our neighbours.

Whilst I cannot provide a worked-through theoretical basis for this new term or concept,[7] I can offer a few pieces, which in their differing ways, challenge us all to be in the business of dramatic theological engagement.

'A Theology of Dramatic Engagement' is based upon the dynamics and challenges of dramatic action – the format or methodology that lies at the heart of this book. The engagement of which I speak relates to the need to enter into the space and the experiences of the 'other'. It is the need to get beyond the rhetoric of polite conversation and instead deal with the messiness of the 'other' through entering into a fictional space that has been created by a facilitator, be they a minister, or an educationist, or a theologian, or all three.

The following pieces, not unlike all the material that precedes them, have been written to encourage (and in some cases force)[8] participants to enter into a fictional space in which they can begin to relate to and reflect upon the experience of others, with a view to examining their own attitudes, and assessing them for their propriety.

Adopting a 'Theology of Dramatic Engagement' (TDE), using the medium of drama and experiential exercises, seeks to respond to the action of God, who in seeking to transform human agency and consciousness, did not opt for a long-range, non-contact approach, but instead opted for a close-at-hand engagement. The Incarnation demonstrates the strategy of God to enter into human history in a dramatic form.[9] The theology of 'presence'[10] is demonstrated by Jesus' engagement with others, through storytelling and dramatic encounter.

In respect of TDE, Jesus' encounter with the Samaritan woman in John chapter 4 is particularly instructive. Jesus finds himself involved in a dramatic encounter with a woman with whom he should not even be speaking. Yet, in this revealing moment, Jesus enters into her experience, inviting the woman to reflect upon her own biography, which leads in turn, to her ultimate transformation.

Clearly, there are limited claims I want to make for TDE within the context of this work. In highlighting the work of Jesus, I am not attempting to link the workings of TDE within a dramatic format with Jesus' ministry. Rather, I want to identify Jesus' actions as an inspiration for the method and approach of TDE within this book.

Grasping the Chaos

Opening reflections

The following sketch was written for the 1st Birmingham All Faiths Day conference for AIDS and HIV. The sketch was a response to a book written by James Woodward.[1] As one of the facilitators and workshop leaders at that conference, I was asked to write a short piece that would invite the participants to reflect upon the attitudes and actions of predominantly Christian people in response to AIDS and HIV.

The conference was held at my home church, Moseley Road Methodist, which is situated in a predominantly multi-ethnic area. The church membership is mainly African Caribbean. I had an instinctive feeling that despite extensive advertisement within the church, few, if any, of the church members would attend the conference. Sadly, my fears came to pass, and aside from a couple of White middle-class members who had remained a part of the church (long after many of their peers had jumped ship, so to speak), none of the (mainly Black) membership attended the event.

As I thought about the piece I was to write, I considered what were some of the reasons why most of the older Black members had chosen not to come. Whilst I disagreed with their reasons, I was sympathetic to many of their fears and concerns. It seemed to me far too easy to write a self-righteous and condemnatory piece berating (Christian) people such as these for their failures, blinkered thinking, and limited action. One's fears do not suddenly evaporate simply because some well-intentioned soul informs you that you should not be afraid. I knew what was going on with this group of people, and I wanted to find a voice that would articulate some of their fears, alongside a counter-presence that would challenge and critique those fears and prejudices.

Once again, the medium of drama and dialogue proved invaluable at this point. For obvious reasons, of all the pieces in this book, this was the hardest one to write. It took me several attempts to locate the appropriate voices and experiences that would bring this piece to life. I felt it important that any character developed should have a sense of integrity in their speech and actions, and must not simply be a cipher through whom one could casually channel one's own anger and frustrations. It is essential that the voices we attribute to people are authentic and speak what we might believe to be the truth.[2]

In re-visiting the following sketch, I have sought to incorporate some of the recent insights from an African context,[3] where the AIDS pandemic is proving to be a potentially greater challenge to the continent than that of slavery or colonialism. I trust that the sketch will challenge all our attitudes and, hopefully, inspire us to greater action.

———◄○►———

Grasping the Chaos

(We see No. 1 sat alone at a table. S/he is reading a newspaper. After a few moments, enter No. 2, who begins to pace around. S/he is clearly agitated. This continues for roughly 30 seconds.)

NO. 1: *(Has finally had enough. Puts down the paper.)* You alright?
NO. 2: *(Stops pacing for a moment)* You asking me if I'm alright?
NO. 1: Unless I'm badly mistaken, I'm sure that's what I said.
NO. 2: Ask me again … Go on, ask me.
NO. 1: Alright … No. 2 … Are you alright?
NO. 2: *(Angry)* No, I bloody well am not!
NO. 1: I take it you're a little upset … Something wrong?
NO. 2: Too right … You bet something is wrong. Something is *very* wrong … *(Nudging No. 1)* … Go on, ask me … Ask me what's wrong.
NO. 1: Alright … No. 2 … Is something wrong?
NO. 2: *(Furious)* You bet there is!
NO. 1: I see … *(Pause)* … Are you going to tell me what's wrong?
(No. 2 begins to pace the room again. After a few seconds, s/he returns to the table.)
NO. 2: You'll never guess what happened, Sunday gone.
NO. 1: You're right … I'll never guess … I'll tell you what, why don't

you just tell me and put us both out of our misery ... What happened?

NO. 2: *(Returns to seat)* I was at church yesterday, right ... Everything was OK. Nothing out of the ordinary was taking place. Then, in comes this man ... The minister introduces this man, and he begins to talk. You'll never believe this. This guy had AIDS ... Yeah, the real McCoy. Can you believe that?

NO. 1: *(Slight pause)* And?

NO. 2: And? And? What more do you want me to say? The guy had AIDS.

NO. 1: AIDS? You sure he said 'AIDS'?

NO. 2: I know what I heard ... Alright, alright, so he didn't say AIDS as such ... It was more ... this HIV positive thing, or something ... But it's all the same thing. Can you believe the minister inviting a person like that into our church?

NO. 1: What's wrong with that?

NO. 2: Are you out of your mind? What's wrong? Didn't you hear what I just said? ... A man with AIDS.

NO. 1: I thought you said it was HIV positive?

NO. 2: Don't be splitting hairs with me ... Same difference ... This man with this disgusting, nasty disease was standing in our church. In front of the pulpit! I hope they disinfected the floor after he'd gone.

NO. 1: I don't believe you. What's your problem?

NO. 2: You must be deaf as well as stupid. I just told you ... This man had AIDS ... HIV, then ... Whatever ... He had no right being in our church.

NO. 1: Why not?

NO. 2: *(Shaking his head)* I don't believe you ... A nasty, infected, diseased man stands in my church, lecturing us on the need to be tolerant, caring and understanding, and you ask what is wrong?

NO. 1: I see his words didn't have any effect upon you.

NO. 2: What?

NO. 1: Tolerant, caring, understanding? No one could accidentally apply those words to you.

NO. 2: Look, smarty-pants ... You don't go to church, so you wouldn't understand ... I go to church to get peace. The church is my sanctuary, it's my spiritual home. I go to church to get away from the hassles and stresses of the world. It's my refuge. I don't want the world to come into my church with its problems and nastiness. I don't want no AIDS person infecting my church.

NO. 1: I'm glad I don't go to your church … I'm not a church person, but do you think it's responsible to cut yourself off from the real world like that?

NO. 2: Of course … We are asked to be *in* the world, but not *of* it.

NO. 1: So that makes it alright to separate yourself?

NO. 2: Yes.

NO. 1: But isn't that unchristian? Cutting people off like that?

NO. 2: *(Smiles)* You know nothing about Christianity, my friend … Let me explain it to you … In all things, there is right and wrong. There is good and bad. Light and dark. Sheep and goats. Christians are asked to be Christ-like. We are asked to have no truck with evil and sin.

NO. 1: *(Slight pause)* So I take it, then, that you are implying that people with AIDS and HIV are sinful people?

NO. 2: You're beginning to catch on.

NO. 1: So these people, because they are sinful, should not be inside the church?

NO. 2: Got it in one!

NO. 1: But what about you?

NO. 2: What about me?

NO. 1: Aren't you sinful?

NO. 2: No.

NO. 1: So you're perfect, then?

NO. 2: I didn't say that …

NO. 1: If you're not sinful, then you must be perfect … Like Jesus … So you're like Jesus?

NO. 2: Of course not … I am sinful … I know what you're driving at … My sins are not the same as these people's.

NO. 1: They're not?

NO. 2: No.

NO. 1: So how are they different?

NO. 2: Mine are little sins.

NO. 1: And HIV and AIDS is a big sin?

NO. 2: Yes.

NO. 1: But I thought all sins were the same. Sin was sin.

NO. 2: No … Well, yes … Look … Some things are worse than others. Some things can be forgiven, others cannot.

NO. 1: Really?

NO. 2: Yes ... *(Looking at No. 1 intently)* ... I must say, I don't like your tone. You don't feel sorry for these people, do you?

NO. 1: I thought it was Christian ... *no*, I thought it was a natural human reaction to feel compassion and sympathy, even empathy if you can manage it, for those less fortunate than yourself.

NO. 2: Not for people like that.

NO. 1: And why not?

NO. 2: Because ... Because ... Just because.

NO. 1: I think you can do better than that. If you're going to be bigoted and prejudiced, at least you can have the decency to put some sense and logic into it.

NO. 2: Because ...

NO. 1: Yes?

NO. 2: Well ... Well ... Because they got what they deserved. You can't feel sorry for people who bring their own misfortune down upon themselves.

NO. 1: So they've asked for it?

NO. 2: Yes ...

NO. 1: What kind of person asks for suffering, fear, loneliness, alienation, pain ...? I could go on. Who would be stupid enough to ask for all that?

NO. 2: You're forgetting that people can be very stupid.

NO. 1: *(Looking No. 2 up and down)* No, I haven't forgotten ... *(Rises to his/her feet and begins to walk around)* ... What about forgiveness for all people?

NO. 2: They don't deserve forgiveness.

NO. 1: Who said only they needed forgiveness? Do you deserve to be forgiven?

NO. 2: God can't forgive them.

NO. 1: You mean you can't forgive?

NO. 2: God can't.

NO. 1: But I thought God was omnipotent. Surely God can do anything?

NO. 2: God chooses not to ... They have transgressed his law. You disobey God and you forfeit his love.

NO. 1: So God only loves people who do exactly what they are told or expected to do? That's a funny kind of love!

NO. 2: You just don't understand, do you?

NO. 1: *(Furious)* You're right … I don't. I don't understand how you can call yourself a Christian, express love for a God you've never seen, but you can be so callous to those who live amongst you.

NO. 2: They don't live amongst me.

NO. 1: How do you know?

NO. 2: I don't know people like that.

NO. 1: How do you know?

NO. 2: I just know …

NO. 1: *(Pause, whilst he thinks)* … You want life to be simple, don't you?

NO. 2: But it has to be. I need life to be simple. I need to believe in good and bad. Innocent and guilty. I can't cope with confusion and muddle.

NO. 1: But life *is* confusion and muddle. Life is one big mass of chaos. Chaos is everywhere. Chaos is in everything. To survive, you've got to grasp it. You have to grasp the chaos.

NO. 2: That's easy to say. Where would we be without order? Life would be impossible … It would be too difficult to bear.

NO. 1: Who said that life should be easy? Life is crazy, varied, strange and chaotic. The only thing that makes sense is love. Love of God. Love for other people … Surely that's what it's all about?

NO. 2: I can't love people who have that thing …

NO. 1: You can say the word.

NO. 2: You know what I'm talking about … I can't, I just can't.

NO. 1: You can try.

NO. 2: It's no good. I can't do it. I can't handle chaos, and I certainly cannot grasp it.

NO. 1: So you would turn your back on your fellow human beings?

NO. 2: I can't deal with them.

NO. 1: So you can't deal with me?

NO. 2: What?

NO. 1: *(Approaches No. 2)* Work it out … Try and make sense of it.
(Exit No. 1 … No. 2 is left alone.)

NO. 2: What did s/he mean? … *(Shakes his/her head)* … I don't understand. It doesn't make any sense. Nothing makes any sense. Nothing …

THE END

———◄○►———

Post-sketch reflections

Two issues have arisen from the piloting of this sketch with different groups across the country. In the first instance, many have speculated on the identity of character No. 1. He/she is a very sympathetic individual whose own identity or position appears somewhat ambiguous. Does s/he have HIV/AIDS? If so, then how did s/he contract it? When these questions have arisen, my first response has been to ask, 'Does it matter?' For some, it does matter, and as this work is primarily about enabling people to ask critical questions of Christianity and faith practice (and not about coercing or guiding people into a particular form of belief), I have to engage with their sense that this particular line of inquiry is important.

For others, their concern has focused on the disparity between the two speakers. Character No. 1 appears not to be a member of a church, and yet in many respects seems to be a more sympathetic and generous person than character No. 2, who is a Christian and does belong to a faith community. This caused a number of people to ask critical questions about Christian action or praxis. Who is the more genuine believer?

Those in the latter camp have pointed to the parable of the Good Samaritan[4] as a prime example of someone outside the traditional religious or 'accepted' framework of belief who is used as an exemplar of 'doing the right thing', as opposed to those who are within that code, but do not.

For those who have exhibited the first response, I have noted a form of 'contractual compassion'. By this, I mean their response to the two characters in the sketch is coloured by the position of character No. 1. If he or she is gay or a lesbian or an intravenous drug user, for example, then this knowledge has a major impact upon their resulting response. It is not that there is no sense of compassion or kindness directed to character No. 1 (if he or she is gay, which has resulted in them contracting the virus)[5] and other people who are suffering with HIV/AIDS, but their response is affected to some extent by this possible knowledge.

What has been most affirming and creative from these encounters has not been the usual theological divide between so-called Liberals and Evangelicals around issues of sin, judgement and orthodoxy versus praxis; rather, it has been the attempts many have made to try and understand and respond better.

In this respect, the work of a number of North American theologians and educators has been most instructive. Gary Gunderson uses the insights of an interfaith health programme in Atlanta to illustrate how congregations can share ideas and experiences in order to support and be in solidarity with those who are broken and suffering.[6] I have found Gunderson's notion of the Church as sanctuary or a 'safe space' to be particularly apposite in the context of these reflections.[7] The notion of the Church as safe or hospitable space is one that is utilised in the ecumenical report on children in the Church, entitled *Unfinished Business*.[8]

Charles Foster has done much to raise our awareness of the need for congregations to create educational models to assist in the task of trying to construct communities that can handle diversity and conflict in a creative fashion.[9] In a collaborative piece of work with Theodore Brelsford, Foster has undertaken case study research, highlighting the differing (and successful) approaches of a number of churches engaging with issues of difference, and how plural communities of faith learn how to celebrate their diversity.[10] The challenge at the heart of *Grasping The Chaos* is one of hospitality and inclusivity. How can churches become safe, hospitable spaces where those who are vulnerable and broken can find a welcoming home? In respect to this central defining issue, Foster writes:

> The movement from messages of hostility to hospitality is required for congregations seeking to embrace the strangers they find in their communities. The difference is seen in comparing the posture of the Prodigal Son's father – standing out on the road expectantly waiting – to the posture of the sulking brother, refusing to participate in the banquet.[11]

The challenge for all of us is to learn to live out the generosity of spirit that is displayed by the father to his son in this famous passage. As this sketch hopefully demonstrates, which is reflected in the various scholarly texts written on this theme, this generosity is ultimately a gift of grace, for it often runs contrary to what we would normally want or choose to do.

Follow-up questions

Read John 9:1–25.

• The disciples assumed that the man was blind due to his sin, but Jesus says that his condition was not of his or God's making. So why are many people suffering with AIDS/HIV? Who is at fault?

• What has been/would be the reaction if a person with AIDS/HIV became a regular worshipper in your church?

• It is often said that 'God has no hands, except our hands'. If that is true, then how can we be a healing presence for people dealing with AIDS/HIV?

• Are there any similarities between the sceptical attitudes of the Pharisees in the passage and character No. 2 in the sketch? If yes, then what are they? If no, then why not?

• With which character do you most identify (and why?)

• Character No. 1 seems very ambiguous in many ways. What do you make of him/her?

• Think of one practical piece of action you and/or your church can do to respond to this issue. Construct a timeline in which this action will be undertaken. What will happen in the next month, the next 3, 6, 12, 18 months etc.?

Issues for the City

Opening reflections

I have lived all my life in the city. I was born in a city, left home to go to another city and currently reside in that same city. I am an urban child, and until attending the annual Methodist Conference in 1996, it had never occurred to me that living in a city might be seen as being a negative experience. At that conference a report was issued which looked at the contemporary state of cities in Britain. Much of the conversation that followed the introduction of the report seemed inherently negative or apologetic.

The tendency within contemporary Christian thought to perceive the city in largely negative terms is due not only to the myriad social and economic problems that exist in these settings, but is also an in-dication of the largely pastoral/rural images that have informed Christian thinking. In John's Gospel, reference to Jesus as a Good Shepherd (John 10:1–18) may have become an essential spiritual and theological truth, but in terms of being a helpful image, if we are honest, it largely functions as a piece of rhetoric for many of us. Sheep and shepherds do not mean a great deal to many of us in our present contexts.

Similarly, when in Psalm 23 the writer states that the Lord is his shepherd who will lead him by green pastures and still waters, this is the ideal tranquil image for aiding and sustaining Christian reflection, and not the bustling vibrancy of the city.

Let's face it – cities get a raw deal in much of our biblical witness. Large conurbations (perhaps the ancient equivalent of our cities) of the Near East era, such as Nineveh or Sodom, do not conjure up positive images in our mind.

A number of writers have attempted to redeem our image of the city, by claiming for it a significant position in God's continuing plan to win back all creation, which God first brought into being.[1] John Vincent in particular has done much to challenge our perceptions and commitment to the modern city.[2] Nor can I forget the prophetic challenge of the Church of England's landmark report *Faith in the City*, which proved its importance simply by being identified as Marxist by a then prominent Conservative cabinet minister.[3]

What I have always treasured about cities, particularly large metropolitan centres, is the fact that they are so conspicuously plural. They are built on difference. Difference is a crucial component in modern Britain.[4] Growing up in Bradford, West Yorkshire, and now living in Birmingham, I have always felt normal in these places. The worst excesses of *Daily Mail*-inspired middle England do not hold sway in these areas. For me, this reality speaks of the multi-cultural glories of Pentecost, when the vibrant plural centre that was Jerusalem witnessed the wild outpouring of God's grace and transformative power.[5]

The following dialogue is my attempt to put forward a positive case for the city as beloved of God and not a setting to be pitied, viewed as being inherently troubling, or one from which we should seek to escape (at the earliest possible opportunity).

———◄○►———

Issues for the City[6]

(We see a man/woman standing centre stage, with thumb in air, trying to hitch a lift. At an opposite end of the stage stands another person, who has a large piece of paper in hand, on which are the words, 'This way to the city'. Person No. 1 is leaving the city. After a few seconds, Person No. 2 approaches No. 1.)

NO. 1: *(To No. 2, who is still trying to hitch a lift)* If you don't mind me asking, where are you going?

NO. 2: *(Melodramatic)* I've had enough … I can't take it any more. I'm sick and tired, tired and sick. Sick and tired, sick, sick, sick, sick of it all.

NO. 1: Not happy, huh?

NO. 2: You bet I'm not. How could you tell?

NO. 1: Lucky guess, I suppose. So what are you sick about?

NO. 2: The city, what else? I can't take that awful, disgusting place any more. I've had enough. I'm leaving. All the best people are leaving. If you've got any sense, you can't stay in the city these days. I'm leaving all the social and economic problems behind. The crime, the unemployment, the stress, the hassle, the community relations, the poverty. I've had enough. I'm heading for the promised land. A place where the beautiful and sensible people live. A place where the air is clear, the environment is more pleasant and the whole atmosphere is so serene, with not a care in the world.

NO. 1: And pray tell, where is this non-city-like community that is heaven on earth?

NO. 2: Evesham⁷ ... I'm going to Evesham in the country. The lush, beautiful countryside of the Vale of Evesham.

NO. 1: *(Slight pause)* ... I see. No disrespect to Evesham – very nice place, I'm sure. Heard good things about it. But not everyone is leaving the city. Not all the movers and shakers are moving out. In my part of the city, they're building yuppy flats and professional townhouses. It's getting to the point where poor people can't afford to live in their long-established communities any more. They've been priced out of the market. Thousands of other people, both rich and poor, Black and White, have lived in the city all their lives, and have no intention of moving. Not everyone wants to live in heaven on earth – even if it is as serene as Evesham.

NO. 2: That's as may be, but you have to admit that the city is a pretty violent place these days. Muggings, robbery, rape, murder ... I could go on. Look what happened to that lovely vicar who was killed on the doorstep of his vicarage in Liverpool a number of years ago. What was his name again? Chris Gray? If a dog collar can't protect you, then there's no hope for any of us.

NO. 1: You're right, there is a cost to living in the city. It can be stressful. Yes, there is crime. But there is stress and crime everywhere. And there are lots of good things happening in the city.

NO. 2: Name some.

NO. 1: There is a solidarity in the city. Ministers and lay people, Black and White, are all struggling together. All are trying to create a space for themselves and their families. You'll find there is a significant amount of friendship, community forums, networks, activism, self-help, mutuality and co-operation. It's all there, in the city.

NO. 2: OK. But apart from the friendship, the community forums, the networks, the activism, the self-help, the mutuality and the co-operation, what else does the city have to offer?

NO. 1: *(Looking at No. 2)* You really have set your heart on Evesham, haven't you?

NO. 2: *(Angry)* Look, you've got to admit that the city is a pretty ugly and depressing place to be. All that concrete, graffiti, dirt, grime and smog. The lack of greenery and the absence of any beauty. The city is a sad, bad and downright ugly place to know.

NO. 1: Do the words 'urban regeneration' mean nothing to you? The city is being renewed. They are changing the way many of our communities look. Capital projects are bringing a new beauty and dignity to our city. Of course, not everyone is convinced about this process. Some would prefer that money were spent on people, offering jobs and status to those who are marginalised and dis-possessed. But we all know how much better we feel about ourselves when the environment in which we live is pleasant and uplifting ... *(Slight pause)* ... Think about some of our drab church buildings. Think about the worst church you've ever been in. What did it look and feel like?

NO. 2: Dry rot, dry people, damp, peeling paint, cold! The whole atmosphere was heavy, like an oppressive weight was pressing down on your shoulders.

NO. 1: Now think of the best. You want a church to be welcoming, bright, warm, well lit, colourful and attractive to look at. These could be the same feelings in and around the city.

NO. 2: Then there's the multi-cultural, multi-faith, multi-this and multi-that, political correctness stuff that the city is full of. Everywhere you go, you see people who don't look like you, people who dress or talk differently from you. The city is full of that.

NO. 1: Great, isn't it?

NO. 2: What? Are you kidding?

NO. 1: Look around you! Look at many of our leading churches. Look at the people. Look at how vibrant and different many of our churches are. If you look at the media, for example ... *(Thinks for moment and then quickly changes his/her mind)* ... Alright, so the media is not a good example in terms of how it portrays the Church and the city. We can't all live in Vicar-of-Dibley-land. It isn't really representative of the communities we are a part of. But out there, in the real world, in the city, there is a great variety of people. People of all faiths. People of no faith. Differing cultures, traditions and practices. Trying to hold all these differences together can be difficult. We can't pretend it isn't. But think of the exciting learning opportunities as we try.

NO. 2: A White boy joined my son's class last month. That makes three. What do you think of that, then?

NO. 1: Think what he'll learn from the others. The city is a great learning environment.

NO. 2: Look, I don't care what you say – the city doesn't stand a chance. There is no hope, nothing to hold onto. The churches have all gone. Even the few that are left are only kept open by people travelling in for one hour on a Sunday. The Church isn't stupid. The Church knows that the city is a lost cause. That's why most of them have closed down, and all the Christians have left.

NO. 1: Gone to Evesham, no doubt … Never heard of the Multi-Racial Projects Fund and the Church of England's Church Urban Fund? These funds support a wide variety of important work in the city – work with national organisations such as the Joint Council for the Welfare of Immigrants and the Howard League for Penal Reform; work within Methodist circuits and Anglican parishes and in Baptist, URC or Pentecostal churches, and in other settings also. These faith communities fund and support community and youth workers in many inner-city settings across the country. What about the number of projects and initiatives that exist and gain their sustenance in the city? In the hard, difficult and often depressing places, the Church is still there. It's not as strong or as vital as many of us would like, but faithful and committed people remain in the city, living out their faith there as best they can.

NO. 2: I hear they've converted my old church, right in the heart of the city … (Slight pause) … They sell carpets there now … Or has it become a temple, or a mosque … (Raising his/her voice) … Why doesn't God do something about the city?

NO. 1: God is! And you staying in the city could make that difference. God could work through you. It is for you to show people the difference, and to recognise God's Spirit at work in his city, and to work with him … (Pause) … Still going to Evesham?

NO. 2: *(Stubborn)* I'm thinking about it.

NO. 1: Let me know when you've decided. There's plenty of work to do in the city. Happy thinking!

NO. 2: Yeah, right. Happy thinking? Now you've got my brain working overtime. I've got to try and figure this one out.

NO. 1: Well, that's part of the challenge of being a Christian. Discerning God's will and going with it. Good luck. See you in ... *(Slight pause)* ... Evesham?

THE END

Post-sketch reflections

When I have used this dramatic dialogue with groups, it has been interesting to note the differing perspectives offered by White participants and Black ones. For the latter, they have immediately latched onto the presence of character No. 1 in the sketch. He/she seems determined to escape. Black participants often possess an implicit 'hermeneutic of suspicion' – an approach to any discourse (whether in text or in oral speech) that is critical, and seeks to read into any conversation suspicions about whose interests are being served by any resulting statement or particular utterance.[8]

Many of the Black participants, using their own experiences as a starting point, expressed their suspicions at the motives of character No. 1 in the sketch. Some felt that their strident determination to leave the city hid their true motives. Namely, their motivation was one of 'White flight'. Their desire to leave is fuelled by a sense of wanting to vacate the city because it had been 'taken over' by Black people. Commentators such as Wilkinson[9] and Nelson,[10] as far back as the mid 1980s and early 1990s, charted the struggles experienced by many White Christians to engage with and work in unity with their Black brothers and sisters in Christ within multi-ethnic urban contexts.[11]

It has been fascinating to witness the number of Black participants saying, 'We know what this person is up to.' Conversely, a number of White people have asserted that, whilst they may not necessarily agree with the sentiments of character No. 2, they nonetheless want to refute the notion that, firstly, he or she is White (a clear presumption of the Black participants) and that he or she is on the 'run'.

As I have read the many texts concerned with urban theology in Britain, I have been struck by the marked reluctance of a number of White scholars to own the reality of 'White flight'. Published works by the likes of Green,[12] Leech[13] and Vincent,[14] aside from concentrating almost exclusively upon the subjectivity and experience of White working-class people, make little reference to the tendency of White people to want to escape from being around Black folk!

Quite naturally, given the set-up of the sketch, character No. 1 dominates the proceedings. In the discussions that have followed the performance of this sketch, character No. 1 has almost always been the centre of attention. The assumption by the Black participants that No. 1 is White reflects not only the operational antenna of suspicion that resides in African Caribbean culture, but is also reflective of a form of critique levelled at the alleged generic nature of Whiteness.[15]

Westfield argues that such is the nature of White privilege that many White people are unable to function when they are placed in radically shifting contexts where their 'taken for granted' notions of superiority are suddenly challenged.[16] It was interesting to note the clear disparity between Black and White readings of this sketch. It will be interesting to see whether these differences emerge when other cross-cultural groups have an opportunity to engage with this piece.

Follow-up questions

Read Acts 2:1–42.

• Make a list of all the different names, nationalities or ethnicities present in Jerusalem at this event. Using a map, try and find these places.

• What do all these different nationalities and cultures tell you about this event?

• With which of the two characters do you most identify in the dialogue? (And why? Or why not?)

• What excites or depresses you about some/many of our cities?

• What can be done to bring new energy, vitality and hope to our cities?

- Reflecting upon the Acts passage and the sketch, what can we learn from the story of Pentecost for our contemporary situation in most modern cities?
- From your reading of Acts chapter 2, what would you say to the two characters in the dialogue?

The Plain Old Honest Truth?

Opening reflections

As a Black Christian educator and a Black liberation theologian I have always believed that notions of balance, objectivity and neutrality are not only severely overrated, but in many cases, are profoundly untrue. When I was a youth and community worker, one of my favourite analogies for explaining the importance of Black theology and the idea that God sides with oppressed Black peoples, was a mythical tale of the encounter between God and two men involved in a struggle on a pavement.

God sees the two men struggling with one another. One of the people fighting is a strong White man who has his foot on the neck of a Black man, who is pinned to the floor. Both men recognise God and call out to God. The White man, with his foot on the Black man's neck, asks God for the strength to continue doing God's will and work by subduing this Black savage. The Black man, conversely, asks for God to intervene and to save him from possible death. God replies by saying that neutrality and objectivity is all important and as such, God cannot intervene or take sides.

When recounting this tale, I usually ask the group, 'Which person is most content with this response from God?' The answer, of course, is 'the person who is most advantaged by the status quo' – the one who is being oppressed would have good reason to doubt the goodness of God in such circumstances.[1]

So why have I told you this tale? Well, mainly due to my motivation for writing the following sketch. *The Plain Old Honest Truth?* is a very unsophisticated and brutal attack upon a particular version of Christianity that is becoming increasingly common. I wrote this sketch after staying with a friend who attends a well-known Black-majority church in London where this form of theology is very popular. This theology is sometimes caricatured as the 'name it and claim it' gospel. My friend not only attends this church, but they also watch a number of the religious channels on a well-known satellite broadcaster, which pumps out a great deal of this unbalanced and, quite frankly, unchristian rubbish.

You see, I am not pretending to be balanced! I was angered and challenged by these programmes. I thought back to my formative experiences in Bradford, as a poor Black inner-city youth. We were poor, and our poverty had nothing to do with the hard work or other-wise of my parents. We were poor due to the structural inequalities and racism of British society. For those who peddle this distorted doctrine, my family simply did not pray hard enough or work sufficiently hard to earn God's favour. Can I live with an idea of God that is neutral about the charlatans who pollute the air with such racist and capitalistic distortions of God's word?

I was appalled at the way in which the speakers on the television programmes manipulated not only the people attending their meetings (many of whom were poor and very vulnerable), but also the Gospel of Jesus Christ. The poor and oppressed, whose lot in life is so often one of abject poverty and absurd nothingness, are, quite naturally, vulnerable to this kind of shameless exploitation.

Robert Beckford, a leading Black British cultural critic and theologian, has written on this issue and states:

> Prosperity doctrines have nurtured an interest in finance and living debt free in many deprived communities in America and Britain. It is right to direct people to the fact that God will meet their needs, including their financial needs. The problem is that 'need' has exploded into legitimation of materialism in Black Churches, so that sacrifice, sharing and suffering have been banished from the meaning of the cross.[2]

When I wrote the following sketch I was incensed by the shameless exploitation of the needs, cares and concerns of poor and marginalised people by slick, North American-influenced capitalists who use the Gospel for their own materialistic empire-driven ends. The likes of

Beckford and McConnell[3] challenge the basic flaws and distortions of capitalistic, money-driven approaches to Christianity that distort the message of Jesus.

In attacking the prosperity-driven approaches to Christianity, it is not my intention to somehow glorify economic and material poverty as being intrinsically a good thing. Quite naturally, we all want to progress and develop as individuals, communities, societies and nations. Alternative approaches to empowering and supporting the poor and excluded have been forwarded by scholars such as Ron Nathan[4] and Paulette Haughton.[5]

I suspect that many of you will feel that I have been unfair on those who fall within this particular tradition of contemporary Christianity. Surely the issue is much more complicated than the sketch that follows? Yes, of course it is, but you have to begin somewhere. And most caricatures begin with a kernel of truth. What is the truth of the Gospel in our present age regarding wealth, the accumulation of material goods and those who are denied even the basics?

————◦————

The Plain Old Honest Truth?

(The scene is a revival meeting. On stage alone there is an evangelist [No. 1] giving his testimony. The crowd are listening intently. The man begins to speak, at first very slowly and then with increased vigour and passion.)

NO. 1: Good ladies and gentlemen, lend me your ears, your hearts and your minds ... For my story is a sad one. I was born the fifteenth of twenty children. Our family was poor ... Yes, we were poor. We were so poor that all twenty of us lived in a shoe-box with the dog, and the dog was incontinent ... Yes, folks, we were poor ... My father worked twenty-eight hours a day just trying to support our family and make ends meet ... *(Begins to sob)* ... When I was three I left school to work with Ma and Pa on the plantation ... Golly, we were poor ... My father died when I was five, Ma quickly followed two years later ... Times were hard. I took me a wife when I reached ten years old and got myself another job to support my wife and the six kids we then had ... *(Pauses for a moment to think)* ... I never did fathom out this birth-control nonsense ... (*Begins to raise his hand in triumph and his voice rises in volume. Real ham acting stuff.*) Then the Lord took a hold of my life and he turned it upside down and me round and round ... He spun me so fast that I got dizzy and I threw up all over his angel who was standing next to me ... The Lord gave me things ... Many, many things. So many things, I just lost count. A Mercedes car, a swimming pool, a yacht, a beautiful wife, complete with plastic surgery and a fixed Barbie-doll smile. He gave me a mansion, a large expenses account and new designer Italian hand-made suits ... (*Pointing to the audience excitedly*) ... And he can do the same for you, my dear brothers and sisters ... He surely can ... All you gotta do is pray to the Lord and say ... 'Lord ...' – 'cos that's his name – 'Lord, I beseech thee, give me riches beyond my wildest dreams. Make mine enemies envious at the mere sight of my deep, rich sun-tan and hand-made suits ... Lord, give me as much money as there are grains of sand on the beach ... Lord, baby, give it to me now ...' (*Calmly now, looking at the audience intently*) ... All you gotta do is to believe in the Lord, that he can give you these things, and give your last hundred pounds to me ... Yep, that's the way it goes, folks. Give me your last pony and I'll pray to big 'G' on your behalf and you'll make back your investment a thousand-fold ... So come on, my little cuties, what do you say? Who's going to be the first one to book himself onto the freedom and glory-bound train to Richville City, Arizona, where all the inhabitants are wealthy, perfectly formed, tanned individuals, who have all got lumbago, due to the heaviness of the wallets they cart around ... Come, folks, who's going to be the first?

(*Absolute silence follows. People are not quite sure about this special offer. After a short interval, one man/woman stands up in the audience and shouts very loudly.*)

NO. 2: What a load of cobblers!

NO. 1: (*Laughing nervously upon hearing this outburst*) I see Satan has sent a viper in our midst, to hinder the work of the Lord ... (*Talking directly to the individual*) ... And what is your name, brother/sister, so that we can pray for your long-lost soul?

NO. 2: (*Very angry*) Don't give that garbage! ... You're a fraud and a con merchant ... You should be ashamed of yourself!

NO. 1: (*Still smiling very confidently, talking directly to the man/woman again*) Would you like to come forward, brother/sister, and share your objections with all these good Christian people?

(*The person slowly begins to make his/her way forward.*)

NO. 1: Lord, I'd ask that you'd heal the heart of this deranged sinner who is slowly making his/her way forward to the podium ... I'd ask, Lord, that you'll drive the devil clean out of his/her heart and that you'll make him/her more like me, Lord ... A kind, obedient saint who serves you as best as I am able.

(*The individual has now made his/her way to the front and is on stage with the evangelist. He/she walks forward and confronts the audience.*)

NO. 2: (*Shouting earnestly*) Don't trust him ... He's a con merchant! He only wants your money.

NO. 1: (*Interrupting No. 2*) That just ain't true, folks ... I want your souls, not ya money ... Money doesn't interest me ... I'm into people, not cold, hard, beautiful, tingling, seductive, crisp, hard, cold money ... (*Thinks upon that for a while and quickly corrects himself*) ... Yes, folks, I'm a person kind of man, not a money man.

NO. 2: (*Looking to No. 1*) Alright, if that's the case ... You won't mind giving me that expensive-looking watch you're wearing, will you?

NO. 1: (*Still smiling but only just*) Of course I will, son ... Of course you can have my little diddy watch ... No problem, but you got to become a Christian first.

NO. 2: (*Smiling merrily*) I am a Christian.

NO. 1: (*A little taken aback*) Yes ... Well, ermm ... You can have my watch tomorrow ... I'm using it now.

NO. 2: (*Beginning to taunt him*) Oh come, come, you're not telling me that a man of your wealth cannot afford to spare one watch? You must have hundreds! (*Placing his/her hand over No. 1's wrist*) ... Go on, let's have it!

NO. 1: (*Irritable, slapping No. 2's hand*) Get off, you ruffian ... (*Raising his right arm in the air*) ... Get thee behind me, Satan!

(*No. 2 is looking into the air at where No. 1 is pointing.*)

NO. 2: (*Trying not to laugh*) Where's this Satan geezer you keep talking about? I'm sorry, but I don't see him anywhere ... Damn elusive fellow, isn't he?

NO. 1 (*Becoming increasingly angry, pointing at No. 2*) You! You are the devil ... I see the devil standing before me. The prince of darkness ... Now be gone from our sight, Mephistopheles!

NO. 2: *(Laughing out loud)* Mephistopheles? Me! The devil? Don't make me laugh … Look, all you see before you is one poor individual, who would like his rich Christian brother – that's you – to share a little of his wondrous riches, given to him by God, with someone less fortunate than himself … Now that doesn't sound too unreasonable, does it? After all, it is the Christian way … *(A short period of silence)* … So what do you say, brother? Give us your watch … One Christian to another!

NO. 1: *(Seething with anger)* Look, it isn't that easy … I can't give you my watch, just like that … I can't!

NO. 2: *(Calmly)* And why not? … *(Patronisingly placing his hand onto the offending wrist with the watch)* … Look, all you've got to do is unbuckle the strap, nice and slowly, and then take off the watch, and then give it to me, who doesn't have a watch … Now, isn't that all so very simple, so easy, that even a simple-minded cretin like you could manage it? So what do you say?

NO. 1: *(Looking up to the heavens for inspiration)* Smite them down, Lord, smite them! Your loyal and humble servant requests it.

NO. 2: *(Also looking up to the heavens for inspiration)* Won't do you any good, you know! Besides, why are you looking up there, when I'm standing right next to you? … *(Quickly nudging No. 1 in the ribs)* … Go on, give us your watch … You won't miss it. Think what a good witness it will be!

NO. 1: *(Looking up to the heavens again and shaking his fist)* Lord! Rid me of this irritant! He/she brings shame on your most honourable and beautiful of names. Lord, consume him/her in an almighty vat of oil.

NO. 2: *(Shaking his/her head thoughtfully)* I get the distinct impression that you don't like me … In fact, I sense a little hostility here … Is anything the matter? Can I counsel you in any way?

(Infuriated by that last suggestion, No. 1 jumps up and down in anger.)

NO. 1: You counsel me? *You* – a disgusting, no-good heathen – counsel *me*? I'll have you know that I have walked with the Lord for over 40 years! What on earth could you teach me?

NO. 2: *(Smiling quietly)* Generosity! Humility! Meekness! Love! I suppose they'll do for starters.

NO. 1: *(Furious, ranting and raving)* You insolent young pup! I'll show you. Counsel me, would you? I'll show you some counselling. Here's a lesson you'll never forget … *(Shouting out to the audience)* Clyde, Lawrence, get your butts over here immediately!

(Clyde and Lawrence come running frantically out of the audience and join the other two on stage. No. 1 begins to lecture them both.)

NO. 1: Listen up, guys, and listen good. I want you two to take this miserable creature outside, slap him up a bit and generally teach him the basic points of respecting your elders and betters. When you've finished doing that, donate the remaining bits of his body to medical research.

(The two men grab No. 2 by the arms.)

NO. 1: *(Begins to laugh)* Counsel me, would you? Have my watch, would you? Hah, that'll show you, you little miserable apology of a human being. You filthy, miserable communist. You deceiver of people and enemy of Christ. Go on, get outta here. Get this miserable wretch outta my sight!

(With this both Clyde and Lawrence begin to drag No. 2 away. As they are about to leave, No. 2 turns around to look at No. 1 again. He/she smiles.)

NO. 2: *(Innocently)* Does this mean that I don't get the watch?

NO. 1: *(Still angry)* Get that miserable creature out of my sight! … Miserable dog … *(Smiling once more, arms outstretched)* … Good ladies and gentlemen … I come before you now, as a humble servant of God … A person who has been touched by Christ. I love each and every one of you … Please turn to the Lord now, before it is too late … God loves you and so do I … Give me your money today, and I will pray for you all … Amen.

THE END

———◄○►———

Post-sketch reflections

This sketch has been viewed with a mixture of hostility and irritation by a number of participants who have engaged with it. The reasons for the anger in some cases have been their reaction to the polemical nature of the sketch as a whole and the attitude of character No. 2

in the drama. A number of participants have felt that my writing is unfair in terms of how I have depicted the two characters.

A number of people have argued that character No. 1 is much too extreme an individual to be taken seriously. Some have argued that economic success and development is all a part of God's providence and abundant generosity. Without wishing to appear either defensive or overly tetchy, I have felt obliged to draw attention to the 'God Channel' on satellite television or the work of well-known speakers such as Creflo Dollar[6] or Joyce Meyer.[7] The latter is one of the leading exponents of a type of ministry that emphasises the abundant, overflowing generosity of God, which includes financial blessings.

Whilst my depiction is undeniably harsh and is very much an extreme caricature, I stand by the piece, as the examples of this form of ministry are very often living cartoon figures in the flesh. This is an extreme piece and character No. 1 is a trenchant figure, but given the extreme nature of this form of ministry and the claims they make for themselves and for God, I think it warrants the kind of treatment I have given it in this sketch. Those who still feel I have been overly harsh on the proponents of this form of ministry would cite such apparent 'proof' texts as 'The blessing of the Lord, it maketh rich',[8] or would point to biblical figures such as Abraham (Gen. 13:2; 24:35), Solomon (1 Kings 10:23), Hezekiah (2 Kings 20:12–18), Job (Job 1:3) and Joseph of Arimathaea (Matt. 27:57). These individuals are all examples of wealthy believers blessed by God.

If I am honest, the polemical nature of this piece and my touchy attempts to defend it against those who have challenged my position, perhaps reveal more about me than they do about those who have opposed my arguments. I did not realise the extent to which this form of ministry raises my emotional and theological hackles until it was brought to my attention that I have satirised this form of Christian practice in a previous piece.[9]

So I am very touchy and transparently biased in my approach to this form of Christian ministry. What has been interesting, in retrospect, is the affirmation I have received from some quarters in response to this piece. Others have felt that I have not been strong enough in my depiction of character No. 1 in the sketch, who, for many, represents the very worst example of Christian-inspired, North American globalisation.

This form of globalisation has become almost as much a homogeneous brand commodity sweeping through the poorer countries of the world as Coca Cola or McDonalds.[10]

The challenges thrown up by prosperity teaching are real. The Black and Liberation theologians who have most shaped my own work, such as Cone,[11] Beckford[12] and Balasuriya,[13] continue to inspire me to hold out for a critical form of Christianity that does not exploit the poor, or offer them false hopes for the eradication of their economic problems. The form of Christianity I am holding out for is a critical one that challenges believers and adherents to be in solidarity with others in order to be co-creators with God in transforming the world, rather than focusing on the narrow and limited gains for the individual.[14] So am I still angry, bitter and frustrated? You betcha!

Follow-up questions

Read Matthew 25:14–30.
- In what way does the attitude of the 'master' in the passage support that of No. 1 in the sketch? Are there any differences?
- The passage seems to endorse wealth creation and material gain. In what way does the reward given to the first two servants justify the approach of No. 1 in the sketch?
- Do you have any sympathy for the third servant in the passage?
- In what ways are the third servant in the passage and No. 2 in the sketch similar?
- Many people would say that the third servant in the passage and No. 2 in the sketch are at best naïve (in their attitude and approach) and at worst are lazy, lacking in initiative, and deserve all that happens to them. What do you think?
- Some have argued that material gain sits very naturally with the Gospel, for life is built upon reciprocal agreements. Work for pay, qualifications for increased salaries, greater salaries for higher mort-gages and better homes, higher pension contributions for more comfortable retirements, faith in Christ for the promise of salvation, and so on. What do you think?
- Given that we do not know what motivated the first two servants (was it fear of punishment or the enticement of reward?), how do we

compare our lives to their actions, and those of No. 1 in the sketch?

- What are the priorities many of us have in our lives? What motivates us to act or behave in particular ways? What kind of rewards are we expecting or looking forward to receiving?

Notes

Introduction

1. This development, however, will be recounted in my forthcoming book, *Dramatizing Theologies: A Participative Approach to Black God-Talk* (London, Equinox, 2006).
2. Anthony G. Reddie, 'Telling A New Story: Reconfiguring Christian Education for the Challenges of the 21st Century' in Dennis Bates (ed.), *Religion, Reconciliation and Inclusion in a Pluralistic World: Essays in Religious Education and Practical Theology in Honour of John M. Hull* (London, Falmer, 2005).
3. I have detailed this phenomenon in some of my previous work, in which I speak of the term 'cultural dissonance'. See Anthony G. Reddie, *Faith, Stories and the Experience of Black Elders: Singing the Lord's Song in a Strange Land* London, Jessica Kingsley, 2001). See also Anthony G. Reddie, *Nobodies to Somebodies: A Practical Theology for Education and Liberation* (Peterborough, Epworth Press, 2003), pp. 97–9, 105–6.
4. See Jerome W. Berryman, *Godly Play: An Imaginative Approach to Religious Education* (Minneapolis, Augsburg-Fortress, 1995).
5. That detailed work is contained in the forthcoming 'sequel' to this book, *Dramatizing Theologies* (op.cit.).
6. Jeff Astley (ed.), *Learning in the Way: Research and Reflection on Adult Christian Education* (Leominster, Gracewing, 2000), pp. 135–7.

How to Use this Material

1. The two exceptions might be *The Quest for Racial Justice*, which is the longest piece in the book and may not be suitable for more than one performance, and the exercise *Stakeholding* which, as it is not a sketch, will need to be handled differently.
2. See Thomas H. Groome, *Sharing Faith: A Comprehensive Approach to Religious Education and Pastoral Ministries* (San Francisco, Harper-San Francisco, 1991) and *Christian Religious Education: Sharing Our Story and Vision* (San Francisco, Jossey-Bass, 1999 [first published 1980]).
3. Jerome W. Berryman, *Godly Play: An Imaginative Approach to Religious Education* (Minneapolis, Augsburg, 1995 [first published in 1991 by Harper-San Francisco]).

SECTION 1 (introduction)

1. See Anthony G. Reddie, *Nobodies to Somebodies* (Peterborough, Epworth Press, 2003), pp. 132–40.
2. Walter Wangerin Jr, *The Book of God: The Bible as a novel* (Grand Rapids, Michigan, Zondervan Books, 1996).
3. Mike Coles, *The Bible in Cockney* (Oxford, Bible Reading Fellowship, 2001).
4. P. K. McCrary, *The Black Bible Chronicles: From Genesis to the Promised land* (New York, African American Family Press, 1993) and *The Black Bible Chronicles: Rappin' with Jesus* (New York, African American Family Press, 1994).
5. Jeff Anderson and Mike Maddox, *The Lion Graphic Bible* (London, Lion Publishing, 1998).
6. See J. Saward, *Perfect Fools* (Oxford, Oxford University Press, 1990). See also H. Lewin (ed.), *A Community of Clowns* (Geneva, WCC, 1987).
7. See Kenneth Leech, *Care and Conflict* (London, DLT, 1990).
8. The group was 'Rise 'n' Shine'. It existed from 1987 to 1991 and performed at the annual Greenbelt Christian Arts Festival for a number of years, winning a prize in the Fringe in 1991. The core members of the group were Charles (Chas) Bayfield, Rupert Kaye and Anthony Reddie.
9. Kenneth Leech, *Through Our Long Exile* (London, DLT, 2001).
10. Augustus Boal, *Theatre of the Oppressed* (London, Routledge, 1982). The work of Augustus Boal will be analysed in greater detail in my follow-up book, *Dramatizing Theologies: A Participative Approach to Black God-Talk* (London, Equinox, 2006).
11. 1 Corinthians 1:20–25.

Bestseller

1. The college at which I am based is the Queen's Foundation for Ecumenical Theological Education, located in Edgbaston, Birmingham. The Foundation has three constituent parts, which are the College (largely full-time residential training for ordained ministry), the Course (largely part-time, non-residential training for ordained ministry) and the research centre. I am based in the research centre. For more details see the Queen's website, www.queens.ac.uk
2. See James H. Cone, *A Black Theology of Liberation* (Maryknoll, New York, Orbis books, 1990), pp. 110–28. See also Jacquelyn Grant, *White Women's Christ, Black Women's Jesus* (Atlanta, Scholar's Press, 1989), pp. 205–22.
3. See Rene Girard, *The Scapegoat*, trans. Yvonne Freccero (London, Athlone, 1986). See also Rene Girard, *Violence and the Sacred*, trans. Patrick Gregory (London, Athlone, 1988).
4. See Kelly Brown Douglas, *The Black Christ* (Maryknoll, New York, Orbis Books, 1993).
5. James H. Cone, *God of the Oppressed* (San Francisco, Harper-San Francisco, 1975), pp. 108–95.

6. JoAnne Marie Terrell, *Power in the Blood?: The Cross in the African American Experience* (Maryknoll, New York, Orbis Books, 1998).

7. Ibid., p. 34.

8. See Robert Beckford, *Jesus is Dread* (London, DLT, 1998) and Riggins R. Earl Jr, *Dark Salutations* (Harrisburg, PA, Trinity Press Interantional, 2001), pp. 1–16.

9. See Cain Hope Felder (ed.), *The Original African Heritage Bible Study Bible* (Nashville, Tenn., James C. Winston Publishing Company, 1993), pp. 998–9.

10. See Dwight N. Hopkins, *Introducing – Black Theology of Liberation* (Maryknoll, New York, Orbis Books, 1999), pp. 23–8.

11. Vincent L. Wimbush, *The Bible and African Americans: A Brief History* (Minneapolis, Fortress Press, 2003), pp. 33–62.

12. The prophetic challenge issued by Isaiah in the text, appealing for justice on behalf of the poor and the marginalised, has been seen by Black people as an indication that the prophet is essentially one of them – he identifies with their plight. See Cain Hope Felder (ed.), *The Original African Heritage Bible Study Bible* (Nashville, Tenn., James C. Winston Publishing Company, 1993), pp. 998–1004.

In the Psychiatrist's Chair

1. See Cain Hope Felder (ed.), 'Exodus' in *The Original African Heritage Bible Study Bible* (Nashville, Tenn., James C. Winston Publishing Company, 1993), pp. 85–94, for a Black social and theological reading of Moses as a Black Afro-Asiatic male.

2. See Anthony G. Reddie, 'Pentecost – Dreams and Visions (A Black theological reading of Pentecost)', Maureen Edwards (ed.), *Discovering Christ: Ascension and Pentecost* (Birmingham, IRBA, 2001), pp. 27–42. In this essay I acknowledge Doreen and Neville Lawrence as prophets and leaders of our age.

3. See Anthony G. Reddie, *Faith, Stories and the Experience of Black Elders: Singing the Lord's Song in a Strange Land* (London, Jessica Kingsley, 2001), pp. 65–72.

4. See Riggins R. Earl Jr, *Dark Salutations* (Harrisburg, PA, Trinity Press International, 2001).

5. See Anthony G. Reddie, *Growing into Hope (Vol. 1): Believing and Expecting* (Peterborough, Methodist Publishing House, 1998). See the section entitled 'Heroes', pp. 59–78. See also Anne S. Wimberly, *Soul Stories: African American Christian Education* (Nashville, Tenn., Abingdon Press, 1996). Wimberly's concept of 'Story linking' involves (African American) learners combining their personal narratives with heroic people of faith. The latter are historic and contemporary people who have been inspired by God to achieve major accomplishments for themselves and for others.

6. Jeff Astley (ed.), *Learning in the Way: Research and Reflections on Adult Christian Education* (Leominster, Gracewing, 2000), pp. 1–32. See also his more recent *Ordinary Theology: Looking, Listening and Learning in Theology* (Aldershot, Ashgate, 2002).

7. Grant S. Shockley, 'From Emancipation to transformation to consummation: A Black Perspective', in Marlene Mayr (ed.), *Does the Church Really Want Religious Education?* (Birmingham, Alabama, Religious Education Press, 1988), pp. 221–48.

8. The apparent maleness of God is challenged in my forthcoming book, *Dramatizing Theologies: A Participative Approach to Black God-Talk* (London, Equinox, 2006).

9. See Robert E. Hood, *Must God Remain Greek?: God Talk and Afro-cultures* (Minneapolis, Fortress Press, 1990).

10. This issue is explored in more detail in my forthcoming book, *Dramatizing Theologies* (op. cit.).

11. See Anthony G. Reddie, *Nobodies to Somebodies: A Practical Theology for Education and Liberation* (Peterborough, Epworth Press, 2003), pp. 132–40.

A Run of Bad Luck

1. Charles F. Melchert, *Wise Teaching: Biblical Wisdom and Educational Ministry* (Harrisburg, Pennsylvania, Trinity Press International, 1998), pp. 74–111.

2. See James H. Cone, *God of the Oppressed* (San Francisco, HarperCollins, 1975).

3. See Jacquelyn Grant, *White Women's Christ and Black Women's Jesus* (Atlanta, Scholar's Press, 1989).

4. Although many actually believe this – after all, isn't that what God has done to Job? Is not suffering simply an example of God's will?

5. William R. Jones, *Is God a White Racist?: A Preamble to Black Theology* (Boston, Beacon Press, 1998 [first published in 1973]).

6. Anthony B. Pinn, *Why Lord?* (New York, Continuum, 1995).

7. A performance poet whose lyrical words are fused with the rhythms of reggae music. A socio-cultural and theological reading of the work of Linton 'Kwesi' Johnson can be found in Robert Beckford, *God of the Rahtid* (London, DLT, 2001), pp. 47–59.

8. Linton 'Kwesi' Johnson, 'Tings and Times' on the *Tings and Times* album (London, LKJ Records, 1991).

9. Harold Dean Trulear, 'African American Religious Education' in Barbara Wilkerson (ed.), *Multicultural Religious Education* (Birmingham, Alabama, Religious Education Press, 1997), pp. 178–82.

10. See Peter J. Paris, *The Social Teaching of the Black Church* (Philadelphia, Fortress Press, 1985) and *The Spirituality of African Peoples: The Search for a common moral discourse* (Minneapolis, Fortress Press, 1995).

11. See JoAnne Marie Terrell, *Power in the Blood?: The Cross in the African American Experience* (Maryknoll, New York, Orbis Books, 1998), pp. 71–98.

12. Matthew 16:24.

13. For a useful examination of Black religious experience see Charles R. Foster and Fred Smith (eds.), *Black Religious Experience: Conversations On Double Consciousness and the Work of Grant Shockley* (Nashville, Tenn., Abingdon Press, 2003).

14. See James H. Cone, *God of the Oppressed* (San Francisco: HarperCollins, 1975) and *For My People: Black Theology and the Black Church* (Maryknoll, New York, Orbis Books, 1984).

15. See J. Deotis Roberts, *Liberation and Reconciliation: A Black Theology* (Maryknoll, New York, revised edn, 1994).

16. See Anthony B. Pinn, *Why Lord?* (New York, Continuum, 1995).

17. Victor Anderson, *Beyond Ontological Blackness* (New York, Continuum, 1995).

Psalm 23: A Modern Version for 21st-Century Sceptics

1. See Anthony G. Reddie, *Faith, Stories and the Experience of Black Elders* (London, Jessica Kingsley, 2001).

2. See Katie G. Cannon, *Black Womanist Ethics* (Atlanta, Scholars Press, 1988), pp. 31–76. See also Rosetta E. Ross, *Witnessing and Testifying: Black Women, Religion and Civil Rights* (Minneapolis, Fortress Press, 2003) and Janice E. Hale, *Unbank the Fire* (Baltimore, Johns Hopkins University Press, 1994), pp. 119–34.

3. See Tom Beaudoin, *Virtual Faith: The Irreverent Spiritual Quest of Generation X* (San Francisco: Jossey-Bass Publishers, 1998).

4. One of the most memorable passages in the Methodist Covenant service is: 'I am no longer my own but yours. Put me to what you will, rank me with whom you will; put me to doing, put me to suffering; let me be employed for you or laid aside for you ... I freely and wholeheartedly yield all things to your pleasure and disposal.' *The Methodist Worship Book* (Peterborough, Methodist Publishing House, 1999), p. 290.

5. Tissa Balasuriya, 'Liberation of the Affluent' in *Black Theology: An International Journal* (Vol. 1, No. 1, Nov. 2002), pp. 83–113.

6. See Dennis A. Jacobsen, *Doing Justice: Congregations and Community Organizing* (Minneapolis, Fortress Press, 2001), pp. 1–7.

7. See Anne-Cathrin Jarl, *In Justice: Women and Global Economics* (Minneapolis, Fortress Press, 2001).

8. See the sketch *The Plain Old Honest Truth* in Section 4, 'Ethics/Action'.

Complaints

1. See David Udo, 'The Necessity to Change From "His-story" to "Our History"' in the First Connexional Conference for Young Black Methodists, *To Overcome is to Undertake* (2–4 November 1990) (London, the Methodist Church – An Inter-Divisional Report, 1991), pp. 32–40.

2. Randall C. Bailey and Jacquelyn Grant (eds.), *The Recovery of Black Presence: An Interdisciplinary Exploration* (Nashville, Tenn., Abingdon Press, 1995), pp. 25–36.

3. Gay L. Byron, *Symbolic Blackness and Ethnic Difference in Early Christian Literature* (New York, Routledge, 2002).

4. Cain Hope Felder (ed.), *Stony the Road We Trod: African American Biblical Interpretation* (Minneapolis, Fortress Press, 1991).

5. The first significant positive sense of my own self-worth within the Methodist Church came with the publication of Heather Walton's *A Tree God Planted: Black People in British Methodism* (London, Ethnic Minorities in Methodism Working Group, the Methodist Church, 1985).

6. Mary Prince was a Black slave woman in the 19th century who published her autobiography in 1831 detailing her experiences of hardship, struggle and emancipation. Her book was entitled *The History of Mary Prince, a West Indian Slave. Related by Herself. With a Supplement by the Editor. To Which Is Added, the Narrative of Asa-Asa, a Captured African* (London, F. Westley and A. H. Davis, 1831). Her book was a key text in the Abolitionary movement of the 19th century.

7. See Vincent Caretta (ed.), *Olaudah Equiano: The Interesting Narrative and other writings* (New York and London, Penguin Books, 1995).

8. See Vincent Caretta (ed.), *Letters of the Late Ignatius Sancho, an African* (New York and London, Penguin Books, 1998).

9. See Vincent Caretta (ed.), *Quobina Ottobah Cugoana: Thoughts and Sentiments on the Evil of Slavery* (New York and London, Penguin Books, 1999). I am greatly indebted to the Revd Lorraine Dixon, a former doctoral candidate in theology at the University of Birmingham, for much of this information. Her research was concerned with the Black presence in English churches in the 18th and 19th centuries.

10. Jean Knighton-Fitt's account of the ministry of Theo and Helen Kotze has brought to life the tension that exists when one has to assess the motives of high-profile activists during the liberation struggle in South Africa. See Jean Knighton-Fitt, *Beyond Fear* (Cape Town, Pretext Publishers, 2003).

11. It is interesting to note the almost saint-like status that is now conferred on Dr Pauline Webb, a former Vice President of the British Methodist Conference, yet she was vilified in some quarters back in the early 1970s for her radical support of (allegedly violent) liberation movements in South Africa. See Colin Morris, 'Profile: Pauline Webb' in *Epworth Review* (Vol. 29, No. 1, Jan. 2002), pp. 13–23.

It Could Have Happened Like This

1. See Lee N. June (ed.), *The Black Family* (Grand Rapids, Michigan, Zondervan Publishing, 1991).

2. See *Black Voices* in the 'Racial Justice' section.

3. See Franz Fannon, *The Wretched of the Earth* (New York, Grove Books, 1984).

4. See Isaac Julien, 'Black Is, Black Ain't: Notes on De-Essentializing Black Identities' in Gina Dent (ed.), *Black Popular Culture* (Seattle, Bay Press, 1992), pp. 255–63.

5. Victor Anderson, *Beyond Ontological Blackness* (New York, Continuum, 1995).

6. See Edward P. Wimberly, *Moving From Shame to Self Worth: Preaching and Pastoral Care* (Nashville, Tenn., Abingdon Press, 1999).

7. See Audre Lorde, *The Black Unicorn* (New York, W. W. Norton, 1995).

8. See Robert Beckford, *God of the Rahtid* (London, DLT, 2001).

9. Doreen Morrison attempts to outline a process where Black people in Britain can begin to challenge the externalised threat posed by racism, whilst still addressing the internalised issues of self-negation and intra-communal dissention within their communities. See Doreen Morrsion, 'Resisting Racism: By celebrating "our" Blackness' in *Black Theology: An International Journal* (Vol. 1, No. 1, May 2003), pp. 209–33.

10. The furore that has been levelled at the educationist and newspaper columnist Tony Sewell (who has challenged the conventional wisdom that racism is the main reason for the educational failure of many Black males in the UK) is a good example.

11. This issue is addressed with great clarity by Robert Beckford, *Dread and Pentecostal* (London, SPCK, 2000).

SECTION 2 (introduction)

1. See Jack L. Seymour, 'Holding onto Hope: Addressing Theological Conflict Through Christian Religious Education', *Religious Education* (Vol. 98, No. 3, Summer 2003), pp. 348–64.

2. See Jose R. Irizarry, 'The Religious Educator as Cultural Spec-Actor: Researching Self in Intercultural Pedagogy', *Religious Education* (Vol. 98, No. 3, Summer 2003), pp. 365–81.

3. The importance of Grant Shockley's legacy can be found in my previous book, *Nobodies to Somebodies* (Peterborough, Epworth Press, 2003), pp. 47–8.

4. Grant S. Shockley, 'Black Theology and Religious Education' in Randolph Crump Miller (ed.), *Theologies of Religious Education* (Birmingham, Alabama, Religious Education Press, 1995).

5. See Anthony G. Reddie, 'Facing the Challenge of the Future' in *The Audenshaw Papers No. 2 201*, The Hinksey Network Torquay, August 2002.

6. See Philip Richter and Leslie Francis, *Gone But Not Forgotten* (London, DLT, 1998).

7. See Jeff Astley (ed.), *Learning in the Way: Research and Reflections on Adult Christian Education* (Leominster, Gracewings, 2000), pp. 1–32.

Christian Jargon

1. Faith Development Theory was created by James W. Fowler, whose research was concerned with how people construct and develop faith. Fowler was more concerned with how faith was structured, and the way in which that structure changes in response to events and developmental issues in human growth and experience, rather than the content of faith. (This is often characterised in terms of looking at the 'why of faith' rather than the 'what of faith'.) See James W. Fowler, *Stages of Faith* (San Francisco, Harper San Francisco, 1995).

2. See James W. Fowler, *Stages of Faith* (San Francisco, Harper San Francisco, 1995). See also Craig Dykstra and Sharon Parks, *Faith Development and Fowler* (Birmingham, Alabama, Religious Education Press, 1986); James W. Fowler, K.

E. Nipkow and Friedrich Schweitzer (eds.), *Stages of Faith and Religious Development: Implications for Church, Education and Society* (London, SCM Press, 1992).

3. See Paulo Freire, *Pedagogy of Hope* (New York, Continuum, 1999). See also James A. Banks (ed.), *Multicultural Education: Transformative Knowledge and Action* (New York, Teachers College Press, 1996).

4. See my editorial and essays by Josiah Young, Cham Kaur-Mann and Clive Marsh (on aspects of Black and Post-Colonial Christologies) in *Black Theology: An International Journal* (Vol. 2, No. 1, Jan. 2004), pp. 7–9, 11–56.

5. William James, *The Varieties of Religious Experience* (New York, Collier, 1961).

6. Adam Hood, *Baillie, Oman and Macmurray: Experience and religious belief* (Aldershot, Ashgate, 2003).

7. Anthony B. Pinn, *Varieties of African American Religious Experience* (Minneapolis, Fortress Press, 1998). See also *Terror and Triumph: The Nature of Black Religion* (Minneapolis, Fortress Press, 2003).

8. Clive Marsh has quite rightly urged caution around the casual (and often careless) way in which such theological labels (denoting certain camps) are used. The Christian landscape is much more complex and nuanced than these labels seem to suggest. See Clive Marsh, *Christianity in a Post Atheist Age* (London, SCM, 2002) and Clive Marsh, 'Sex, Shopping and other Weighty Theological Matters – Part 2', *Epworth Review* (Vol. 31, No. 2, April 2004), pp. 53–60.

9. See Andrew Walker, *Telling The Story: Gospel, mission and culture* (London, SPCK, 1996).

10. Some comments have accorded with particular ideas developed by the likes of Jacquelyn Grant, *White Women's Christ, Black Women's Jesus* (Atlanta, Scholars' Press, 1989) and Kelly Brown Douglas, *The Black Christ* (New York, Orbis, 1994).

A Problem Shared

1. See Kenneth Leech, *Through Our Long Exile* (London, DLT, 2001).

2. See John Vincent, *Radical Jesus* (Basingstoke, Marshall Pickering, 1986).

3. Gustavo Gutteriez, *A Theology of Liberation* (New York, Orbis, 1973).

4. Leonardo and Clodovis Boff, *Introducing Liberation Theology* (Tunbridge Wells, Burns and Oates, 1987).

5. Emmanuel Y. Lartey, *In Living Colour: An Intercultural Approach to Pastoral Care and Counselling* (London, Jessica Kingsley, 2003).

6. See Charles R. Foster and Theodore Brelsford, *We Are the Church Together* (Valley Forge, Pennsylvania, Trinity Press International, 1996), pp. 17–40.

7. See John Munsey Turner, *Methodism, Revolution and social change* (Wesley Historical Society, West Midlands Branch, 1973); Ted Jennings, *Good News to the poor: John Wesley's Evangelical Economics* (Nashville, Tenn., Abingdon, 1990). See also David Hempton, *The Religion of the People: Methodism and popular religion* (London, Routledge, 1996).

8. Rupert E. Davies, *Methodism* (Peterborough, Epworth Press, 1985), pp. 56–104.

9. See Philip Cliff, *The Rise and Development of the Sunday School Movement in*

England 1780–1980 (Birmingham, National Christian Education Council, 1986).

10. Clive Marsh acknowledges aspects of this process in the social and cultural development of himself and his family. See Clive Marsh, *Christianity in a Post Atheist Age* (London, SCM Press, 2002), pp. 12–19.

Ministry of the Whole People of God in the World

1. Jeff Astley (ed.), *Learning in the way: Research and Reflections on Adult Christian Education* (Leominster, Gracewings, 2000), pp. 33–71.

2. Grant S. Shockley, 'From Emancipation, to Transformation to Consummation: A Black Perspective' in Marlene Mayr (ed.), *Does The Church Really Want Religious Education?* (Birmingham, Alabama, Religious Education Press, 1988), pp. 221–48.

3. See Theodore W. Jennings Jr, *Good News to the Poor: John Wesley's Evangelical Economics* (Nashville, Tenn., Abingdon Press, 1990); Theodore Runyan, *The New Creation: John Wesley's Theology Today* (Nashville, Tenn., Abingdon Press, 1998).

4. Charles R. Foster and Fred Smith (eds.), *Black Religious Experience: Conversations On Double Consciousness and the Work of Grant Shockley* (Nashville, Tenn., Abingdon Press, 2003).

5. N. Lynne Westfield, *Dear Sisters: A Womanist Practice of Hospitality* (Cleveland, Ohio, Pilgrim Press, 2001).

6. Anne S. Wimberly, *Soul Stories* (Nashville, Tenn., Abingdon Press, 1996).

7. John M. Hull, *What Prevents Christian Adults From Learning?* (London, SCM, 1985).

8. Mary Elizabeth Mulino Moore, *Teaching from the Heart: Theology and Educational Method* (Harrisburg, Pa., Trinity Press International, 1998).

9. Jeff Astley, *Ordinary Theology: Looking, Listening and Learning in Theology* (Aldershot, Ashgate, 2003).

10. See Colleen Birchett, 'A History of Religious Education in the Black Church' in Donald B. Rogers (ed.), *Urban Church Education* (Birmingham, Alabama, Religious Education Press, 1989), pp. 76–9.

11. Philip Luscombe and Esther Shreeve (eds.), *What is a Minister?* (Peterborough, Methodist Publishing House, 2002).

12. See Clive Marsh, 'Priests and Prophets, but not Servants', and Esther Shreeve, 'Collaborative Ministry and the Ministry of the Whole People of God' in Philip Luscombe and Esther Shreeve (eds.), *What is a Minister?* (Peterborough, Methodist Publishing House, 2002).

13. See Marlene Mayr (ed.), *Does the Church Really Want Religious Education?* (Birmingham, Alabama, Religious Education Press, 1988).

SECTION 3 (introduction)

1. Robert Beckford, *Dread and Pentecostal* (London, SPCK, 2000), pp. 67–94.

2. Samuel K. Yeboah, *The Ideology of Racism* (London, Hansib, 1988).

3. President Lyndon B. Johnson signed the Civil Rights legislation on 2 July 1964.

Section 2 of the bill states: 'All persons shall be entitled to the full and equal enjoyment of the goods, services, facilities, privileges, advantages, and accommodations of any place of public accommodation, as defined in this section, without discrimination or segregation on the ground of race, color, religion, or national origin.'

4. See Glynn Gordon-Carter, *An Amazing Journey: The Church of England's Response to Institutional racism* (London, Church House Publishing, 2003). See also Sandra Ackroyd, Marjorie Lewis Cooper and Naboth Muchopa, *Strangers No More* (London, Methodist Church, 2001).

5. Dennis L. Okholm (ed.), *The Gospel in Black and White: Theological Resources for Racial Reconciliation* (Downers Grove, Illinois, InterVarsity Press, 1997).

6. Anthony G. Reddie, *Nobodies to Somebodies* (Peterborough, Epworth, 2003), pp. 156–8.

7. W. E. B. Dubois, *The Souls of Black Folk* (New York, Bantam Books, 1989 [first published in 1903]), p. 3.

Stakeholding

1. The Universal Declaration of Human Rights, proclaimed by the General Assembly of the United Nations on 10 December 1948.

2. Some of these accounts are detailed in Anthony G. Reddie, 'An Unbroken Thread of Experience' in Joan King (ed.), *Family and All That Stuff* (Birmingham, National Christian Education Council, 1998), pp. 153–60.

3. Paul Gilroy, *There Ain't No Black in the Union Jack* (London, Hutchinson, 1987).

4. See Gretchen Gerzina, *Black England: Life Before Emancipation* (London, John Murray, 1995) and Ron Ramdin, *Reimaging Britain: 500 years of Black and Asian History* (London, Pluto Press, 1999).

5. See Bhikhu Parekh, *Rethinking Multiculturalism: Cultural Diversity and Political Theory* (Basingstoke, MacMillan Press, 2000), pp. 195–235.

6. Inderjit S. Bhogal, 'Citizenship' in Anthony G. Reddie (ed.), *Legacy: Anthology in Memory of Jillian Brown* (Peterborough, Methodist Publishing House, 2000), pp. 137–41. See also Inderjit S. Bhogal, *On The Hoof: Theology in Transit* (Sheffield, Penistone Publications, 2001), pp. 69–71.

7. See Anthony G. Reddie, 'Pentecost: Dreams and Visions – A Black Theological Reading' in Maureen Edwards (ed.), *Discovering Christ: Ascension and Pentecost* (Birmingham, IRBA, 2001), pp. 27–42.

8. See Robert Beckford, *God of The Rahtid* (London, DLT, 2001), p. 12.

9. See Matthew 25:31–46, particularly vv. 35 and 38.

10. See Robert Beckford, *Dread and Pentecostal* (London, SPCK, 2000), pp. 73–80.

11. See Sandra Ackroyd, Marjorie Lewis-Cooper and Naboth Muchopa, *Strangers No More: Transformation Through Racial Justice* (London, Methodist Church, 2001) for an analysis of the different forms in which racism is manifested. See also Naboth Muchopa, *Making a Positive Difference* (London, Methodist Church, 2001).

12. See Acts 17:26; Genesis 1:27–28; 3:4; Romans 3:9–21. (2) A God who acts for justice – Psalm 76:7–9; Genesis 4:9–12; Exodus 3:7–11, 20; 14:8. (3) Christ died to free all creation – Romans 8:21; 8:19–22; John 3:16; Matthew 25; Luke 4:18–19. (4) Christ died to create a single humanity – Ephesians 2:11–12; Matthew 12:48–50; 1 Peter 2:9–10; Galatians 3:26–29; Ephesians 2:11–16; Colossians 3. (5) The Kingdom of God is … Justice – Romans 14:17; Matthew 7:15–24; Ephesians 6:10; John 3:18; James 2:1–13; 5:1–6; Isaiah 1:15–16; Amos 5:21–24. (6) The Future Kingdom – Hebrews 11:13–16; Matthew 5:6, 10; Revelation 7:9; 21:1; Acts 10:34–35; Revelation 7:15–17; 2:3–4.

The Quest for Racial Justice

1. The theoretical and technical issues in using this approach to talking about questions of faith and God will be explored in my next book, *Dramatizing Theologies: A Participative Approach to Black God-Talk* (London, Equinox, 2006), where I will be using sketches and dialogues in a more analytical way.
2. Richard Reddie, book review of *Making a Positive Difference* by Naboth Muchopa, *Black Theology: An International Journal* (Vol. 1, No. 1, Nov. 2002), p. 120.
3. Tee Garlington, 'The Eucharist and Racism' in Susan E. Davies and Sister Paul Teresa Hennesee SA (eds.), *Ending Racism in the Church* (Cleveland, Ohio, Pilgrim Press, 1998), pp. 74–80.
4. Ibid., pp. 75–8.
5. E. Hammond Oglesby, *O Lord, Move This Mountain: Racism and Christian Ethics* (St Louis, Chalice Press, 1998).
6. Ibid., p. 8.
7. This phrase refers to the numerous occasions I have witnessed very educated White people attempting to use their intellect to construct spurious and often inane arguments to justify their hidden and subtle racism. It usually takes the form of a convoluted sentence, which begins with the words, 'I hear what you say, and very much agree with you, *but* don't you think …' The words that follow what I have termed the 'infamous but' are, in effect, what the respondent really believes, and contain a concealed attempt to 'catch out' or 'wrong foot' the racial justice trainer or anti-racist theologian. I have learnt to ignore the many words that precede the 'infamous but', as these are mere window-dressing or rhetorical 'flannel'. The true sentiments of the respondent exist in the slippery words that follow the 'but'.

Black Voices

1. See *It Could Have Happened Like This* in Section 1, 'Biblical Re-telling'.
2. See Peter J. Parris, *The Social Teaching of the Black Churches* (Philadelphia, Fortress Press, 1985) and Dale P. Andrews, *Practical Theology for Black Churches* (Louisville, John Knox Press, 2002).
3. Anthony G. Reddie, *Nobodies to Somebodies* (Peterborough, Epworth Press, 2003), pp. 29–36.

4. See Isaac Julien, 'Black Is, Black Ain't: Notes on De-Essentializing Black Identities' in Gina Dent (ed.), *Black Popular Culture* (Seattle, Bay Press, 1992), pp. 255–63.

5. Michael Eric Dyson, *Reflecting Black: African American Cultural Criticism* (Minneapolis, University of Minnesota Press, 1993).

6. Kobena Mercer, *Welcome to the Jungle: New Positions in Black Cultural Studies* (London, Routledge, 1994).

7. Victor Anderson, *Beyond Ontological Blackness: An Essay on African American Cultural Criticism* (New York, Continuum, 1995).

8. Ibid., pp. 118–31.

9. Michael Eric Dyson, *I May Not Get There With You: The True Martin Luther King, Jr* (New York, Simon and Schuster, 1999).

10. Michael Eric Dyson, *Holler If You Hear Me: Searching for Tupac Shakur* (Pittsburg, University of Pennsylvania Press, 2002).

11. See Dennis L. Ockholm (ed.), *The Gospel in Black and White: Theological Resources for Racial Reconciliation* (Downer's Grove, Illinois, InterVarsity Press, 1997).

12. Lerleen Willis, 'All Things to All Men? Or What has Language to Do with Gender and Resistance in the Black Majority Church in Britain?', *Black Theology in Britain* (Vol. 4, No. 2, May 2002), pp. 195–213.

13. Carol Tomlin, *Black Language Style in Sacred and Secular Contexts* (New York, Caribbean Diaspora Press, 1999).

14. Christine Callender, *Education for Empowerment: The Practice and Philosophies of Black teachers* (Stoke-on-Trent, Trentham Books, 1997), pp. 65–95.

15. See Anthony G. Reddie, *Nobodies to Somebodies* (Peterborough, Epworth Press, 2003), pp. 97–9, 105–6.

16. See Jonathan S. Epstein, *Youth Culture: Identity in a Post Modern World* (Oxford, Blackwell, 1998).

17. The BBC programme *The Real McCoy* was a very popular Black comedy sketch show which emerged in the early 1990s. Since the demise of this show, individual comedians such as Curtis Walker, Angie Le Mar and Felix Dexter have emerged as major comedians on the separate and distinct Black comedy circuit in the UK.

18. See Robert S. Beckford, *Jesus is Dread* (London, DLT, 1998). See also his *Dread and Pentecostal* (London, SPCK, 2000).

19. Robert S. Beckford, 'Theology in the Age of Crack: Crack Age, Prosperity Doctrine and "Being There"', *Black Theology in Britain: A Journal of Contextual Praxis* (Vol. 4, No. 1, Nov. 2001), pp. 9–24.

SECTION 4 (introduction)

1. Anthony G. Reddie, *Nobodies to Somebodies* (Peterborough, Epworth Press, 2003). See the section entitled 'A Theology of Good Intentions'.

2. See Anthony G. Reddie, *Nobodies to Somebodies* (Peterborough, Epworth Press, 2003).

3. The term and the concept that accompanies it will be explored in greater detail in my forthcoming book, *Dramatizing Theologies: A Participative Approach to Black God-Talk* (London, Equinox, 2006).

4. Some of my initial thinking has been inspired by Jose Irizarry. See Jose R. Irizarry, 'The Religious Educator as Cultural Spec-Actor: Researching Self in Intercultural Pedagogy', *Religious Education* (Vol. 98, No. 3, Summer 2003). pp. 365–81.

5. See Anthony G. Reddie, *Faith, Stories and the Experience of Black Elders* (London, Jessica Kingsley, 2001).

6. See Cain Hope Felder (ed.), *Stony the Road We Trod* (Minneapolis, Fortress Press, 1991), pp. 127–86 and Vincent L. Wimbush, *The Bible and African Americans* (Minneapolis, Fortress Press, 2003).

7. This concept will be refined and expanded in my next book, *Dramatizing Theologies* (op. cit.).

8. Only to a certain extent can this be true, for if particular individuals are wholly resistant to any educational context, there is not much any educator or facilitator can do.

9. See James H. Cone, *A Black Theology of Liberation* (Maryknoll, New York, 1990), pp. 110–28. See also Jacquelyn Grant, *White Women's Christ and Black Women's Jesus* (Atlanta, Scholars' Press, 1989), pp. 194–222.

10. Robert S. Beckford, 'Theology in the Age of Crack: Crack Age, Prosperity Doctrine and "Being There"', *Black Theology in Britain: A Journal of Contextual Praxis* (Vol. 4, No. 1, Nov. 2001), pp. 9–24.

Grasping the Chaos

1. See James Woodward, *Embracing the Chaos: Theological Responses to AIDS* (London, SPCK, 1990).

2. Womanist theologians (Black women who talk of God in light of their experiences) such as Delores Williams and Katie Cannon argue that the authenticity of the Black women's voice is essential for the development of any form of theological reflection that will be relevant for their contexts and experiences. See Delores S. Williams, *Sisters in the Wilderness* (Maryknoll, New York, Orbis Books, 1993) and Katie G. Cannon, *Black Womanist Ethics* (Atlanta, Scholars Press, 1988).

3. Paul J. Issak, 'Health and Healing As A Challenge to Christian Ethics and Diaconal Ministry of the Church', *Black Theology: An International Journal* (Vol. 1, No. 2, May 2003), pp. 161–73.

4. Luke 10:25–37. See the sketch *The Quest for Racial Justice* in Section 3 and the study questions that accompany it. I have used this passage from Luke to aid individuals and groups in their reflections.

5. The fact that this is unnamed in the sketch, and yet people have speculated upon it and constructed their whole response on this speculative 'fact', only serves to remind us of the ways in which individuals and groups 'read' their own experiences into any text.

6. See Gary Gunderson, *Deeply Woven Roots: Improving the Quality of Life in Your Community* (Minneapolis, Fortress Press, 1997).
7. Gary Gunderson, *Deeply Woven Roots: Improving the Quality of Life in Your Community* (Minneapolis, Fortress Press, 1997), pp. 83–92.
8. *Unfinished Business: Children and the churches*, commissioned by the Consultative Group on Ministry among Children (CGMC) (London, CCBI Publications, 1995).
9. See Charles R. Foster, *Educating Congregations: the Future of Christian Education* (Nashville, Tenn., Abingdon, 1994).
10. See Charles R. Foster and Theodore Brelsford, *We Are the Church Together: Cultural Diversity in Congregational Life* (Valley Forge, PA., Trinity Press International, 1996).
11. Charles R. Foster, *Embracing Diversity: Leadership in Multicultural Congregations* (Herndon, VA, Alban Institute, 1998), p. 57.

Issues for the City

1. See *The Impact of the Global: An Urban Theology* (London, Anglican Urban Network, 2001). Also Michael Northcott (ed.), *Urban Theology: A Reader* (London, Cassell, 1998) and Kenneth Leech, *Through Our Long Exile* (London, DLT, 2001).
2. See John Vincent, *Hope from the City* (Peterborough, Epworth Press, 2000) and Christopher Rowland and John Vincent (eds.), *Gospel From The City* (Sheffield, UTU, 1997).
3. *Faith In the City: The Archbishop's Commission on Urban Priority Areas* (London: Church House Publications, 1985).
4. See *The Parekh Report: The Future of Multi-Ethnic Britain* (London, Profile Books, 2000).
5. See Robert Beckford, *Dread and Pentecostal* (London, SPCK, 2000), pp. 168–76. Also Cheryl Bridges Johns, *Pentecostal Formation: A Pedagogy Amongst the Oppressed* (Sheffield, Sheffield Academic Press, 1998), pp. 62–110 and Anthony G. Reddie, 'Pentecost: Dreams and Visions – A Black Theological Reading' in Maureen Edwards (ed.), *Discovering Christ: Ascension and Pentecost* (Birmingham, IRBA, 2001), pp. 27–42.
6. This sketch was inspired by a conversation with Revd Anthony G. Malcolm, who is a Methodist minister.
7. When using this sketch, please feel free to change the name of the location that provides the heaven-like idyll for No. 1. Evesham is simply an example for Midlands (Birmingham, in particular) participants. Choose any location that represents the type of suburban or rural ideal to which urban people might want to escape.
8. See Cain Hope Felder, 'The Bible – Re-Contextualisation and the Black Religious Experience' in Gayraud S. Wilmore (ed.), *African American Religious Studies: An Interdisciplinary Anthology* (London and Durham, Duke University Press, 1989), pp. 156–68.

9. See John Wilkinson, 'Inheritors Together' in James H. Evans Jr, John Wilkinson and Renate Wilkinson (eds.), *Inheritors Together – Theology and Racism, No. 2* (London, Race, Pluralism and Community Group, Board For Social Responsibility, 1985), pp. 5–19.
10. Clarice T. Nelson, 'The Churches, Racism and the Inner cities' in Paul Grant and Raj Patel (eds.), *A Time to Speak* (Birmingham, a joint publication of Racial Justice and the Black Theology Working Group, 1990), pp. 3–11.
11. See also John Wilkinson, *Church in Black and White* (Edinburgh, Saint Andrew, 1993).
12. See Laurie Green, *Urban Ministry and the Kingdom of God* (London, SPCK, 2003).
13. Kenneth Leech, *Through Our Long Exile* (London, DLT, 2001).
14. John Vincent, *Hope from the City* (Peterborough, Epworth Press, 2000).
15. See Nancy Lynne Westfield, 'Teaching for Globalized Consciousness: Black Professor, White Student and Shame', *Black Theology: An International Journal* (Vol. 2, No. 1, Jan. 2004), pp. 73–83.
16. Ibid.

The Plain Old Honest Truth?

1. Frederick Ware outlines some of the opposition mounted by some Black theologians to the notion of God being on the side of oppressed Black peoples. Some of these scholars argue that there is no evidence to suggest that God does take sides, and if God does not choose to side with the oppressed, then what is the point of the oppressed believing in God? See Frederick L. Ware, *Methodologies of Black Theology* (Cleveland, Ohio, Pilgrim Press, 2002), pp. 66–114. See also William R. Jones, *Is God a White Racist?: A Preamble to Black Theology* (Boston, Beacon Press, 1998).
2. Robert Beckford, 'Theology in the Age of Crack: Crack Age, Prosperity Doctrine and "Being There"', *Black Theology in Britain: A Journal of Contextual Praxis* (Vol. 4, No. 1, Nov. 2001, Sheffield, Sheffield Academic Press), p. 20.
3. See D. R. McConnell, *A Different Gospel: A Biblical Look at the Word and Faith Movement* (Peabody, MA, Hendrickson, 1988).
4. Ron A. Nathan, 'Prosperity through Empowerment: A Tribute to the late Revd Leon H. Sullivan (1922–2001)', *Black Theology in Britain: A Journal of Contextual Praxis* (Vol. 4, No. 1, Nov. 2001, Sheffield, Sheffield Academic Press), pp. 25–31.
5. Paulette Haughton, 'At the Coalface: Fighting Deprivation' in Michael Simmons (ed.), *Street Credo: Churches in the community* (London, Lemos and Crane, 2000), pp. 75–87.
6. For information see Creflo Dollar Ministries, PO Box 490124, College Park, GA 30349. Website address is www.creflodollarministries.org
7. See www.joycemeyer.org
8. Proverbs 10:22.

9. See Character No. 2 in Anthony G. Reddie, 'Talking To God: A Dramatic Piece on the theme of prayer' in Anthony G. Reddie (ed.), *Legacy: Anthology in memory of Jillian Brown* (Peterborough, Methodist Publishing House, 1998), pp. 146–51.

10. See Simon Coleman, *The Globalisation of Charismatic Christianity: Spreading the Gospel of Prosperity* (Cambridge: Cambridge University Press, 2000).

11. Harry Singleton III, *Black Theology and Ideology: Deideological dimensions in the theology of James H. Cone* (Collegeville, Mn., Liturgical Press, 2002).

12. See Robert Beckford, *God and the Gangs* (London, DLT, 2004).

13. Tissa Balasuriya, *The Eucharist and Human Liberation* (London, SCM Press, 1979).

14. Inderjit S. Bhogal, *A Table for All* (Sheffield, Penistone Publications, 2000), pp. 11–34.